Hoop Tales® Series

SO-FAJ-074

Hoop Tales:

Iowa Hawkeyes Men's Basketball

Buck Turnbull

INSIDERS' GUIDE®

GUILFORD, CONNECTICUT
AN IMPRINT OF THE GLOBE PEQUOT PRESS

INSIDERS' GUIDE®

Text design: Casey Shain

All photos are courtesy of the University of Iowa Sports Information Office, unless otherwise noted.

Cover photos: *front cover:* Jeff Horner (photo by Harry Baumert, © 2006, The Des Moines Register and Tribune Company. Reprinted with permission); *back cover:* top, Kevin Kunnert; bottom, B. J. Armstrong

Library of Congress Cataloging-in-Publication Data is available.

ISBN-13: 978-0-7627-4317-9
ISBN-10: 0-7627-4317-4

Manufactured in the United States of America
First Edition/First Printing

Contents

To all the Bumblebees.
If you're a Hawkeye fan who proudly wears the Black and Gold,
this book is for you.

Acknowledgments

I would like to thank Phil Haddy, University of Iowa sports information director, and his associate director, Steve Roe, for their help and support in this project. And a special thanks to their secretary, Theresa Walenta, for helping me choose a good cross-section of photos. Most of the photos featured in this volume are from the files of Iowa's Sports Information Office.

I would also like to thank once again my computer guru, son Gary Turnbull, for helping to solve several minor crises. I think I've finally graduated into the twenty-first century, using these newfangled machines with a fair amount of confidence now.

Also, thanks to George Wine, Bob Brooks, Susan Harman, Charlie Mason, Les Steenlage, and Harold Yeglin for their contributions to my research.

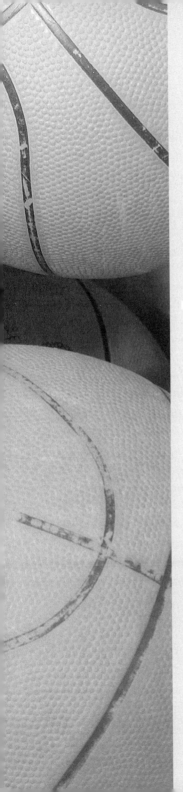

The Fieldhouse

It was called simply the Fieldhouse. Or the Iowa Fieldhouse if you want to get technical. That was it. No name of a wealthy donor on the brick wall outside. No worthy person to be honored for posterity. Just the Field-house.

But what a place it was—and still is, for that matter, sitting atop the Grand Avenue hill of Iowa's west campus in mute testimony to all the thrilling basketball games that were played there on cold winter nights so many years ago. Now the excitement has moved to nearby Carver-Hawkeye Arena and all that's left from the old days are wonderful memories: From the acrobatic shooting of little Murray Wier to the dominant play of big Chuck Darling, and from the incredible shooting of "Downtown" Freddie Brown to the magical play of Ronnie Lester, many of the brightest stars in Iowa's past gained lasting fame in the Fieldhouse.

Three Hall of Fame coaches, Sam Barry, Ralph Miller, and Lute Olson, plied their trade there. And two others, Lawrence "Pops" Harrison and Frank "Bucky" O'Connor, became celebrity figures in Iowa by guiding their teams to Big Ten championships.

Mention the Fieldhouse to Hawkeye old-timers and watch their eyes glaze over. Or maybe they'll cover their ears in memory of all the deafening roars that greeted one of Wier's impossible shots that somehow dropped through the net, or the foot stomping in the balcony that gave noisy support to the home team and had to drive visitors to distraction.

You might think sitting on board planks on the lower level or steel seats in the balcony or being stuck behind a pillar would have kept fans away, but on the contrary, they showed up no matter what the discomforts were. Sometimes the students were there four hours before the tip-off just to make sure they got in. The building's capacity was about 13,500, but it was taxed to overflowing many times. "The Fieldhouse wasn't very comfortable," recalls Wier, "and it definitely wasn't comfortable for the other team. I spent some of the best times of my life in that building. It's hard to describe the atmosphere to someone who never saw a game there, but it was loud, very loud. I loved the place."

A Collegiate First

Although the University of Iowa didn't play its first intercollegiate basketball schedule until the 1901–02 season, notching a 10–2 record under its coach, Ed Rule, the budding sport had its beginnings much earlier than that. Iowa played Chicago in January of 1895 in Close Hall on the university campus. It was claimed to be the first college game west of the Mississippi with five players on a side.

In 1891 a young man named Henry Kallenberg came to Iowa from Springfield, Massachusetts, to study medicine and to serve as the director of the university's YMCA. At Springfield, Kallenberg was well acquainted with James Naismith, who had sought to devise an indoor game that would interest his bored YMCA physical education classes. The game Naismith came up with in the fall of 1891 was a primitive version of what we now call basketball.

Kallenberg obtained a copy of the rules from Naismith and introduced the game to his students during the Christmas break of 1891. There is not much historical data about the origins of the sport at Iowa, but a photograph in the university's *Vidette-Reporter* dated 1892 clearly shows a peach basket nailed to the balcony at one end of the Close Hall gym.

Kallenberg later arranged the game with Chicago, but the newspaper gave no report of any final score, saying only that the Iowa team lost. Specifying that five players were on each side at any given time was an important detail because Naismith's original rules allowed for as many as forty. If that seems a bit strange, how about this? The game was played with a football! It was thrown from player to player and eventually at the basket, with no running allowed.

Naismith recommended nine players on each side as the ideal number. About the only similarity between his rules and today's game is the height of the baskets. And the reason for the original height was because the balcony at the Springfield YMCA was 10 feet above the floor.

He should have. Nobody enjoyed performing on the home court more than Wier, who lost only twice there in forty-eight games over four years. The 5'8" dynamo (or was he only 5'7"?) led the nation in scoring in 1948, when the Associated Press picked its first All-America team and honored him among the five players chosen.

All three of Iowa's Final Four teams played in the days of the Fieldhouse. Bucky O'Connor coached back-to-back Big Ten champions in 1955 and 1956, teams affectionately remembered as the "Fabulous Five." The second time, they finished runner-up to San Francisco and the great Bill Russell. Although Lute Olson's 1980 Hawkeyes took no better than fourth place in the conference, they surged in the postseason with four straight NCAA tournament victories to make the Final Four.

In 1970 Ralph Miller assembled what many consider Iowa's all-time best team, featuring the brilliant combo of John Johnson and Fred Brown. Those Hawks won the Big Ten title with a perfect 14–0 run, leading the nation in scoring and setting a conference record that still stands with an astounding 102.9 points per game. But Jacksonville's last-second basket in the first round of NCAA play sent them to the sidelines with a disheartening 104–103 loss.

The Fieldhouse was born in the controversial regime of an athletic director named Dr. Paul E. Belting, who was hired in the spring of 1924 to replace Howard Jones, Iowa's highly successful football coach. Jones had also served as the athletic director but didn't particularly enjoy doing any administrative work beyond his football duties. From 1920 to 1923 Jones's teams won a school-record twenty straight games and Big Ten titles with unbeaten teams in 1921 and 1922.

The formidable brick structure known as the Iowa Fieldhouse, as it appeared in the early 1930s.

In late 1923 and early 1924, Jones became embroiled in a dispute with the university's administration, particularly B. J. Lambert, chairman of the athletic board, over the way he directed his department, in addition to the time he would be available to coach football. Basically, Jones had decided he wanted to spend more time at his home in Excello, Ohio, giving up his job as athletic director and coming back to Iowa only for the football season.

Further complicating this picture, university president Walter Jessup had decided it was past time to combine the athletic department and the Department of Physical Education, placing them under the leadership of one man. Well, Jones definitely wanted no part of that, since it would undoubtedly put him under the direction of someone else. So Jones resigned in February 1924, much to the chagrin of some vocal alumni, who felt their football coach was being railroaded out of town. Jones left to coach one year at Trinity University (now Duke) and then headed for the University of Southern California, where he had spectacular teams, winning all five Rose Bowl games in which they played.

Meanwhile, Lambert had also resigned as chairman of Iowa's athletic board, a last-minute move that he hoped would placate Jones. It didn't work, and Jessup suddenly found himself with three or four jobs to fill all at once. The man brought in to be athletic director as well as head of the PE department was Dr. Belting, coming over from the University of Illinois, where he had been a football lineman in 1910 and 1911. Unfortunately, Belting was not very well liked from the beginning because of his ego and headstrong personality.

Belting's choice for football coach was a former Iowan, Burt Ingwersen, who had also played football at Illinois. Hiring two men with Illinois connections did not sit well with some Iowa alums. Even though Ingwersen was from the Iowa border town of Clinton, he was looked on as a turncoat for casting his lot with the Illini. If all this seems like the seeds for trouble, it was—for both Belting and Ingwersen.

One of the first things Belting did was to make a thorough study of Iowa's inadequate athletic facilities, located just east of the Iowa River. The basketball team played in a small gymnasium on grounds down the hill from the Old Capitol, and the football field was just west of that near the river bank. It was quickly determined that both needed to be replaced. And one thing you have to say on Belting's behalf—he might have been unpopular, according to historians, but he was a visionary. There would be no skimping on the size and scope of a new Iowa Fieldhouse, nor would there be on what is now Kinnick Stadium.

During this time—in 1923—Sam Barry coached the Iowa basketball team to its first Big Ten co-championship title, and the Hawks repeated in 1926. By the spring of 1926, work was well under way on construction of the $300,000 Fieldhouse, which was a massive three-pronged structure—a large swimming pool to the south with lanes 50 yards in length, the Fieldhouse proper, and a huge north gymnasium. A dirt-floor armory had been built several years before and that was attached to the building.

When the structure was dedicated at a three-day ceremony on January 13–15, 1927, a printed program handed out at the festivities boasted, "No finer or larger building of its kind has ever been erected in the world." And there might have been a sound basis for the claim, judging by the figures in the program. These were the basic specifications: length from north to south, 464 feet; width from east to west, 430 feet; average height, 60 feet; ground covered, three acres. The Fieldhouse reportedly seated 15,000 and the swimming pool area 3,500. (The Fieldhouse figure was a stretch, even with a later expansion of bleachers taken into consideration.)

Even longtime followers of the Hawkeyes may not know this fact about the north and south balconies of the Fieldhouse: When the new football stadium was built in 1929, seats from old Iowa Field were salvaged and became balcony seating for basketball.

The first game in the Fieldhouse was a 43–13 romp over St. Louis University in early December of 1926, and there is a noteworthy sidelight to that as well. One of the Hawkeye players was future coach Pops Harrison. However, the Hawks were on the other end of a lopsided score in their January dedication game, when a crowd of about 7,500 saw them lose to Michigan, 41–22.

In the meantime, on the football field three straight shutout losses to end the 1925 season and a 3–5 record in the fall of 1926 left Hawkeye fans in turmoil, and a petition was circulated calling for Ingwersen's resignation. And these fans were none too happy with Belting, either, despite his role in bringing the new Fieldhouse into being. It was also during this time that the Big Ten's commissioner, John L. Griffith, had begun investigating charges that Iowa's alumni had for some time been using a slush fund to pay athletes.

Although not known at the time, Belting had transferred a large amount of athletic department money to a downtown bank in Iowa City, apparently to eliminate alumni involvement in dispersing monthly stipends to athletes. The so-called Belting Fund was to be used for loans, some of which were never repaid, of course, while giving the appearance of the arrangement's being entirely legal. Many other universities, especially the large schools in the Big Ten, were apparently involved in such chicanery. Iowa made the mistake of leaving a paper trail. Belting later blamed the alumni for much of the problem, saying they were too heavily involved in Hawkeye athletics.

Then in the spring of 1929, while all these troubles were festering and construction of the new stadium was under way, Belting decided he'd had enough and suddenly resigned. This is how he phrased his feelings in a letter to President Jessup:

> This year I am completing a five year program of educational service as the Director of the Division of Physical Education in the State University of Iowa. Under this new organization, the indebtedness of the old stadium was paid; the Field House was built; the golf course was developed, and the new Stadium was begun and is now under rapid construction . . .
>
> The graduate work in physical education that has been developed under my direction is unsurpassed in any college or university in the United States. The program of intramural games has reached a high point of development, and the intercollegiate teams have achieved distinction. Much of this accomplishment has been paid for out of the careful management of the net proceeds from intercollegiate football.
>
> To this program of achievement I point with pride. Naturally, continued opposition, dissension, and jealousy have developed over a program that not only has moved so rapidly but has had only educational aims in view. I would gladly see the Stadium through to final completion but these dissensions have been embarrassing to the University and disheartening to me.
>
> I therefore tender my resignation to take effect at the completion of this five year program.

Belting's resignation was duly accepted by Iowa's Board in Control of Athletics, and in a matter of days, two university staff members were named to succeed him—Dr. Edward H. Lauer as the new PE director and track coach George Bresnahan as athletic director. However, Belting wasn't quite done. He paid the alumni back for all their meddling by going to the Big Ten spring meetings in Chicago and charging that Iowa did not have proper faculty control of athletics. The alumni were running the show, he said.

Later that year, after Iowa had dedicated its new 43,000-seat stadium (now about 70,000), the Big Ten lowered the boom. Iowa was suspended from the conference for one year, a sentence later reduced to only the month of January 1930. Oh yes, in the midst of all this, Sam Barry decided it was best for him to get out, and he joined Howard Jones at Southern California, earning more distinction and eventually making it into the National Basketball Hall of Fame. Rollie Williams, a former Wisconsin player, took over the Hawkeye basketball job.

This rather detailed synopsis of Iowa's woes heading into the Great Depression of the 1930s helps explain why the Hawkeye football and basketball teams experienced such a difficult decade, probably the worst in their history. The Hawks had these fancy new facilities but were not allowed to play a Big Ten basketball schedule in 1929–30, and only Purdue agreed to meet them in the 1930 football season. Talented athletes who might otherwise have been interested shunned the school, and the aftereffects of the suspension led to some hard times. Burt Ingwersen survived the turmoil despite all the calls for his resignation, but he finally called it quits and left after his 1931 squad won only one game and was walloped by combined scores of 131–7.

Williams's first basketball team struggled to win only four of seventeen games, losing six in a row early and six straight to end the 1930 campaign. Two more losing seasons followed before such players as Howard Moffitt, Howard Bastian, and Ben Selzer finally got them on the winning side with a 15–5 record in 1933 and 13–6 in 1934. Selzer was recognized on several All-America teams as a senior in 1934, and many years later was honored by being named to Iowa's All-Century team.

But it was mostly rough going in the years leading up to World War II. One notable starter on the 1938 team was sophomore Nile Kinnick, who averaged 6.1 points per game as the Hawks scraped out an 11–9 record, going 6–6 in conference games, finishing in a tie for fifth place. Kinnick injured an ankle playing football the following fall and decided to give up basketball. In 1939, of course, he won the Heisman Trophy, and less than four years later, he was killed while on a navy training flight.

Basketball became a much more popular spectator sport when the rules were changed before the 1937–38 season, eliminating the center jump from taking place after every basket. The result was a much faster game, and the Fieldhouse crowds soon grew to 11,000 and more in the conference season. Williams assembled perhaps his finest outfit in the winter of 1941–42, led by Tom Chapman Sr., Milt Kuhl, and Vic Siegel. Those Hawks were 10–5 in conference play to tie for second place, their best showing since the two Big Ten championship teams of the 1920s.

Then the war began to alter the landscape in all sports nationwide. Williams went off to serve in the navy, leaving the coaching reins in the hands of his longtime assistant, fiery Pops Harrison, and although nobody could possibly be aware of it at

Playing inside the packed and noisy Fieldhouse was never easy for visiting teams.

the time, Iowa was heading into its "Golden Era" of basketball. It would take a while, though, because college rosters were undergoing a constant shuffling. Players would be on a team one day, then off to the service the next, perhaps even to a naval collegiate training program, where they would come back to play for a rival team in the same conference.

The Iowa Fieldhouse was taken over and used as a naval training site, with such famed football coaches as Bernie Bierman, Don Faurot, Bud Wilkinson, and Jim Tatum serving there.

A Seventy-Seven-Game Winning Streak

Iowa's basketball teams went for fifteen years without losing a nonconference game in the Iowa Fieldhouse, starting with the season of 1942–43. The winning streak reached seventy-seven games before it was snapped in an 81–68 loss to the University of Washington on December 20, 1958.

Pops Harrison never lost a preconference game at home as head coach. Neither did Bucky O'Connor. Although many of the opponents were not big names, the streak did include occasional victories over the likes of Notre Dame, USC, Kentucky, Nebraska, and Arizona.

So did future Iowa coach Forest Evashevski, who taught hand-to-hand combat. With that lineup of coaching talent, it was only natural that the Iowa Seahawks became one of the best-known and toughest service teams anywhere.

Harrison's first year as the basketball coach was like so many others, the team posting an undistinguished 7–10 record in 1942–43. After that, however, the portly and lively man with the bald dome knew little but success. Dick Ives came in from the small town of Diagonal, preceded by mountains of publicity as an Iowa high school star, and joined two other freshmen as immediate starters—hometown hero Dave Danner, an Iowa City standout, and Jack Spencer, a rail-thin, play-making guard from Davenport. The Fieldhouse would never be the same.

Those three, along with sophomore Ned Postels and senior Lloyd Herwig, didn't lose a game until February 1944, starting off with twelve straight victories. One was a 103–31 rout of hapless Chicago, with Ives going on a 43-point rampage, setting a Big Ten record that lasted for many years. It still ranks third on Iowa's all-time list. Only one player has outdone him in all the following years, John Johnson, who scored 46 points against Wisconsin-Milwaukee in 1968, hiking that record to 49 against Northwestern in 1970.

Harrison's youthful crew finished with a 14–4 overall mark, including 9–3 to tie for second in the conference. Then came the arrival of another highly touted freshman, pint-sized Murray Wier. (Would he be big enough for the rugged Big Ten?) Herb Wilkinson, a transfer who had starred as a rookie on Utah's 1944 national champions, along with older brother Clayton, another gifted player, also joined the team. That's when the real fun began.

Cheap Thrills

When Iowa won its first clear-cut Big Ten championship in 1945, it didn't cost much to watch all the excitement. Reserved seats for Big Ten games sold for $1.00. General admission tickets for all games went for 60 cents, and if you were high school age or younger, the price dropped to 30 cents. Hawkeye students were admitted by merely showing their ID card.

One other gem rates mention because it's an Iowa City legend and a cherished part of Fieldhouse lore. For a number of years before and after World War II, the state high school basketball tournament was played in the Fieldhouse. Some teams were even bedded down in the cavernous upper reaches between the south balcony and the swimming pool, and it was an ideal situation for the youngsters to play pickup games lasting most of the night. Early round tournament games would start at 9:00 A.M. and go to 10:30 P.M.

In the late winter of 1946, an unheralded Iowa City team began to make some noise during tournament week and stormed all the way into the final game, meeting LeMars, from northwest Iowa, for the state championship. The amazing run was seemingly going to end there, however, because LeMars owned a 5-

point lead and the ball with a little more than one minute remaining. But a missed free throw let Iowa City gain possession, and in the next 55 seconds, Bob Freeman became a City High legend by hitting three straight baskets that won the game, 41–40.

One eyewitness said the winning shot was at least as far as the center circle, and the length continued to grow in the retelling until someone claimed "it went past the moon." Far from it, Freeman admitted years later: "The first two were substantial shots from out past the head of the key—not exactly high percentage shots. The third was the length of a free throw."

Freeman lettered as a reserve on Iowa's 1948 team and later became an insurance executive in Des Moines. But for years he couldn't escape the fame of his one glorious minute. When he was introduced to strangers, invariably he would be asked, "Are you the Bob Freeman who . . . ?" Yes, he was, and he never got tired of answering that question.

The Fieldhouse is still the hub of much activity on Iowa's west campus, being totally refurbished after the team's move to Carver-Hawkeye Arena. Intramural games and other forms of recreation are the main focus now, along with intercollegiate swimming and gymnastics meets. But these are obviously much quieter times for the staid old structure.

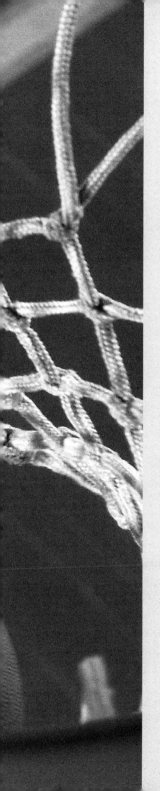

The Little
Redhead

When Murray Wier was a youngster growing up in Grandview, a small community near Muscatine in southeast Iowa, he would shoot baskets behind the family home every chance he got. Sometimes the opportunities were limited, though, because his two older brothers had put up the backyard basket and didn't want little Murray using it.

If they weren't around, he would go out and practice an assortment of crazy shots that eventually would lead to stardom many years down the line. He was always undersized for his age, and he knew early in life that he had to find a way to launch his shots over or around the bigger boys he played against. And after a while those acrobatic, off-balance shots felt completely normal to him. "As I got older, my brothers would let me play in their backyard games," Wier said. "I had to learn running hook shots and stuff like that to get the ball over their heads. Pretty soon this came naturally for me—in fact, I got pretty good with the hook shot. It might have looked awkward but it didn't feel awkward to me. That's just the way I played."

Murray never did grow much taller than 5'7", although when he got to be a consensus All-American at Iowa in 1948, leading the nation in scoring, he was listed at 5'8" and 145 pounds.

The thing that caught the eye about his unusual shooting style was his accuracy. What might have looked like luck the first time or two became accepted as the norm the more his shots went in. Fans would just shake their heads and say, "That's Murray. He can't shoot unless he's off-balance, falling down."

Word of his shooting prowess began to spread beyond Grandview, and Murray told his parents one day, "You've got to get me out of here. We've got to move to Muscatine so I can play ball at a bigger school."

"My mother went in to Muscatine and applied for a job, and when the man interviewing people saw her name on the application, he said, 'Are you related to the Wier who plays basketball?' She said, 'That's my son.' There were no more interviews. She got the job."

At Muscatine, Murray's peculiar style and uncanny shooting ability became a hot topic among coaches and fans in Iowa's high school ranks. As a senior he earned more votes for the all-state

Despite his short stature, Murray Wier's crazy shots and deadly accuracy made him a star at Iowa in the 1940s.

team than any of his much bigger rivals, and while his size might have turned away some college recruiters, one coach who quickly saw unlimited potential in the little redhead was Iowa's Pops Harrison. A short man himself, Harrison had been good enough to play basketball for the Hawkeyes almost twenty years earlier, and he was not going to hold Wier's lack of height against him.

"Outside of my dad, Pops was the most important man in my life," said Murray. "He really looked out for his players and took a personal interest in them. He made me go to class when I might have slacked off otherwise. All I really wanted to do was play basketball. I sometimes wonder where I'd be if it wasn't for him. I probably wouldn't have amounted to much."

There were many detractors who didn't think a youngster of Murray's stature had a chance to make much noise playing among the muscular bruisers of Big Ten basketball, but that only made him more determined to prove them wrong when he signed on with Iowa in the fall of 1944. This was the same year that two standout players, brothers Herb and Clay Wilkinson, transferred from Utah to attend Iowa's dental school—and incidentally play basketball. And it was just a year after one of the most heralded players in Iowa high school history, Dick Ives, had launched his Hawkeye career.

Suddenly Harrison had a wealth of talent. His team had been good the year before, leaping into the limelight with a 14–4 record and vaulting from a ninth-place finish in the Big Ten in 1943 to a tie for second in 1944. That young team featured two other rookie standouts in addition to Ives—Jack Spencer of Davenport and Dave Danner of Iowa City. Danner had a bad back and couldn't play much in the 1944–45 season, but Ives and

Iowa's Noteworthy "First"

Iowa's Dick Culberson was the first African American to play basketball in the Big Ten. Culberson, a little-used reserve from Iowa City, earned a varsity letter on the 1944–45 team that won the conference championship.

Spencer were both classified 4-F in the draft, so World War II was unlikely to hamper the squad.

Harrison's starting five entering the 1945 season included junior Ned Postels along with Ives, Spencer, and the two Wilkinsons. Wier was the sixth man. Herb Wilkinson, a 6'4" guard, was already well known as the player whose basket won the national championship game for Utah in 1944. Clay Wilkinson (6'5") had left Utah to go on a Mormon mission after his freshman season two years before, so both Wilkinsons had three years of eligibility left when they arrived in Iowa City.

It didn't take long for all this talent to come together. The Hawks routed an outclassed Western Illinois team in their opener, 101–23, and the 78-point winning margin remains a school record more than sixty years later. Iowa scored at least 60 points in all six of its nonconference games, and then easily disposed of Minnesota and Purdue at home in early January to start

Big Ten play. Extra seats had to be installed in the Fieldhouse, and a crowd of 12,200 saw the high-flying Hawks crush Purdue, 61–34.

After that one, sports editor Tom Wuriu wrote this glowing praise in the *Iowa City Press-Citizen:* "You can take it for a fact: If Pops' boys play like they did Saturday night consistently, they won't lose a game to anybody, anywhere." But seven of the first eight games had been played at home and the seemingly unbeatable Hawks were in for a rude awakening at Michigan. They trailed the whole game and were behind, 27–22, in the closing minutes when Harrison inserted Wier with instructions to shoot.

And that's when the legend of Murray Wier began to take hold. He scored three straight baskets to put Iowa ahead, 28–27, and the Hawks added one more point on a technical foul to win, 29–27. The technical free throw resulted when Michigan called a timeout it didn't have, and the game ended in mysterious circumstances. One of the Iowa players was knocked unconscious by the timekeeper.

After Wier entered the game as a substitute for Postels, Harrison told Postels to go sit behind the timekeeper to make sure his timing was on the up-and-up. Michigan's antiquated scoreboard clock did not show seconds, only minutes, and the official time was kept at the scorers bench. This naturally could lead to confusion in the last minute, and when the clock didn't start on time after an inbounds pass, Postels tapped the timer on the shoulder and told him to start the clock. Bam! He was flattened by a haymaker. The timer later claimed Postels had grabbed the clock out of his hands, and he was only protecting himself. About the only certainty at the wild finish was that Iowa had won the game.

The next road game was at Illinois, and the Hawks had only themselves to blame for their one loss of the season. They missed 9 of 15 free throws and went down to defeat, 43–42. Six straight conference victories followed and that set up the rematch at home against Illinois to end the regular season. Interest was at fever pitch, of course, and the game was sold out two weeks in advance. A crowd of 14,400 saw Iowa win the showdown, 43–37, to claim the school's first outright Big Ten championship. And that's the way the season would end, with a 17–1 record, because Iowa declined an automatic NCAA tournament bid.

No Tournaments

Although Iowa had a 17-1 record to win the Big Ten title in 1945 and went 14-4 to take third place in 1946, the coach, Pops Harrison, turned down postseason tournament bids both years. He said all his players couldn't get out of school to accept an automatic NCAA berth after winning the conference championship. Second-place Ohio State went instead.

The next year, when the Hawks were 14-2 with two games remaining, Harrison declined a bid to the National Invitational tournament in New York's Madison Square Garden. "I don't know why Pops told us this," said Murray Wier. "It only made the guys mad. In those days the NIT was just as big or bigger than the NCAA. I guess he figured we would win the Big Ten and go to the NCAA, but we lost our last two games. Ohio State went again and we didn't go anywhere."

Native Iowan Dick Ives was another Hawkeye standout in the mid-1940s.

"Pops didn't want to go," Wier maintains. "For some reason, he didn't like tournaments. He used as an excuse that the Wilkinsons were in dental school and couldn't get away, but that wasn't true. I think he was just happy to win the Big Ten, and he didn't want anything to tarnish that."

Harrison had earned himself a salary boost from $3,500 a year to $5,000, and the future never looked brighter for Iowa basketball. But the following season, with most of the same players returning, was a bit of a letdown—a third-place finish in the Big Ten. However, that season remains stuck in Wier's memory bank for one particular shot, which he calls the best of all his many crazy baskets.

"We were playing Minnesota at home and they were good, with guys like Bud Grant and Tony Jaros back from the service," said Wier. "They were in front most of the game and led by 4 points with not much time to go. I made two free throws but still, the game was almost over. Then we got the ball back when they were called for traveling. Postels threw the ball in to me, and right away I saw Ives breaking for the basket. I went up in the air to throw him a pass so he could sweep in for his left-hand shot, but all of a sudden he broke the other way. I was in midair. What could I do? I had no other choice—I just threw the ball at the basket and the darned thing went in.

"It was unbelievable, and naturally the crowd went nuts. That really fired us up and we beat 'em in overtime."

Because of plays like that, Bert McGrane once described Wier this way in the *Des Moines Register*: "He was unguardable. He'd fire 'em off his ear or up from an ankle with equal abandon, even hoisting in baskets from midair in the midst of a dive. He didn't shoot baskets. He threw 'em in while racing, whirling, and engaging in some other means of rapid transit."

Harrison's Hawkeyes, with much of the same cast returning in Wier's junior year, were a major disappointment in 1946–47 and at one point they lost five straight conference games, slipping to sixth place in the final standings with a 7–9 league record. And with the departure of Ives and the two Wilkinsons, little was expected from the 1948 team. But that would be the season that stamped Wier forever in the vanguard of Hawkeye basketball greats. He led the nation in scoring and set a Big Ten record doing so, earning so much national acclaim that he was one of only five players selected when the Associated Press chose its first All-America team.

Bob Schulz, a freshman member of the 1945 championship squad, was back from the service to team with Spencer in an all-Davenport tandem at guard. Transfer Red Metcalfe filled the void at center, with Floyd Magnusson and Bob Vollers trading off at the other forward spot opposite Wier. The Hawks won their first eight games and eleven of thirteen before facing a key test at Purdue. Schulz said he will never forget how Wier fired up his teammates before that game.

"The Purdue varsity lettermen all sat together and they began riding Murray in the pregame warmups," Schulz said. "When we left the floor for the dressing room, he gave them a little obscene gesture, and that really riled them up. After a while, things got pretty quiet in the dressing room, and all of a sudden Murray picked up an orange—one of those oranges that is sliced up to eat at halftime—and he flung it against the wall, yelling, 'I'm tired of losing to these guys over here. Let's go get 'em.'"

As it turned out, he was lucky he got the other Hawks charged up. Since Metcalfe had just flunked out at midyear, Purdue ganged up on Wier and limited him to 5 points, so it was Schulz and reserve center Don Hays who contributed the key baskets that won for Iowa, 41–33.

Then came a game at home against Illinois when Wier poured in a career-high 34 points and was carried from the floor on the shoulders of his joyous teammates after a 70–61 victory. Two more home games remained and Iowa, with a 7–2 conference record, had to win both to remain in title contention with Michigan. The opponents were border rivals Wisconsin and Minnesota, in whose gyms Iowa had suffered its only two league losses. The Wisconsin game had been a particularly hard-fought battle in Madison and afterward one of the Iowa players shouted, "Just wait till we get you in Iowa City."

That comment was picked up by one national magazine in a story telling how rough the sport of basketball had become in the Big Ten, and that school officials were finding it difficult to keep rowdy crowds under control. Wisconsin had a diminutive star of its own in Bobby Cook, who was almost the equal of Wier, but their showdown seemed to be only a sidelight because of the possible riotous conditions that were being predicted. Iowa's athletic brass even went so far as to have the band prepared to play the national anthem if trouble broke out.

Well, as it developed, nothing happened of an untoward nature. There were no unpleasant incidents, only happy cheers from the home fans as Iowa cruised to a 62–40 victory. But the next game was a different story. Minnesota came in with a rugged team, powered by 6'9" center Jim McIntyre, who had scored 36

"Pops" Was for Lollipops

Because former Iowa coach Lawrence "Pops" Harrison was a bald, fatherly type of person, you might think that's how he got his nickname. Not so. He was tagged with that moniker because of his childhood fondness for lollipops. Almost all his life he was called either "Pops" or "Popsy."

When Harrison was ill and dying of cancer in 1967, all his former players were invited back to attend a dinner honoring their popular coach. After Pops had delivered a short speech that resembled one of his old pep talks, each player was given an opportunity to say a few words to him. "Pops, I don't know whether you remember this," said Bob Schulz, a four-year letterman in the Harrison era, "but during one close game in my freshman year, you yelled at me to get up. I thought, 'Oh boy, he's going to put me in.' But what you wanted was my chair—so you could throw it at the officials."

Schulz said Pops had not lost any of his keen wit. Without hesitation, and with a twinkle in his eye, Harrison responded, "Sure, I remember that, Bob. It was the best play you made for me in four years."

From 1943 to 1950 Harrison's Hawkeye teams won 98 games and lost 42. His winning percentage of .700 is the best in school history for those who coached more than four years.

"Pops" Harrison

points (Wier had 30) when the Gophers won the earlier meeting in Minneapolis, 72–56. By the time the teams squared off on a Saturday night in late February, the crowd was already in a frenzy.

"Bob Schulz won that game for us," recalls Wier, who tossed in 28 points. "McInyre scored only 2 points because he got hurt. Early in the game, there was a jump ball and Schulz came down hard on McIntyre's instep. It might have been on purpose, I don't know, but nobody saw it. The officials didn't see it, but McIntyre wasn't the same the rest of the game. Boy, that Schulz was a tough player."

This time the band did have to play "The Star Spangled Banner." A fight broke out in the closing seconds after Schulz came out of a scramble for the ball and threw an elbow that bloodied the lip of Minnesota's Pete Tapsak. Others entered the melee, and it appeared that fans were also getting involved. Someone in street clothes charged into the middle of the fisticuffs, but he was later identified as Bucky Harris, an injured Hawkeye player who did not dress for the game but was sitting on the bench. Officials soon restored order, with the help of the band, and after Schulz and Tapsak were ejected, Iowa went on to win, 54–50.

So it was off to Michigan for the season finale with a share of the conference title on the line for the Hawkeyes, but the Wolverines finished with a 10–2 record by winning, 51–35, and Iowa settled for second at 8–4. It had been a storybook season, however, especially for Wier. He scored 399 points in nineteen games, modest by today's standards, but his 21-point average was the best in the country. "Remember, that was before the three-point shot," Wier said, adding with a laugh, "The guys used to kid me that they'd pass me the ball and wouldn't get it back. If we'd had a three-point shot, I might never have passed the ball."

Those were great times for Wier. After the season he was presented with a convertible and treated to a parade by the hometown fans in Muscatine. He hated to see those glory days come to an end. "The day I picked up my cap and gown for the graduation ceremonies, I went out on the steps, sat down, and started to cry. I couldn't believe how fast the years had gone by. I loved the university and I loved the guys I played with—a great bunch of guys. I knew I was going to miss them. It had been the best time of my life."

Wier played for three seasons in the infancy of professional basketball, first in Moline, Illinois, and then at Waterloo, in north central Iowa, but the game was moving away from smaller cities and into the large metropolitan areas in the 1950s. Murray decided he'd better settle into a stable career, so he became a teacher and coach at East Waterloo High School. He coached there for thirty-eight years, serving as athletic director for thirty-six. His 1974 basketball team won the state championship.

Murray also took up a new career, becoming one of Iowa's most noted senior tennis players, winning numerous age-group events. After a while many junior players couldn't beat him, either. "I had to laugh sometimes when I'd be paired against a younger guy in a tournament," he said. "They'd look at me, this short little gray-haired guy, and I knew they had to think this is going to be a piece of cake. Then I'd whip up on them."

As a retirement gift from East Waterloo, the school's faculty, students, and other friends gave Murray and his wife, Margie, a trip to England's Wimbledon tennis tournament. Several years ago the Wiers moved to a senior community near Austin, Texas, and at the age of eighty Murray was still playing tennis five times a week.

His days as a basketball star may be in the distant past, but to old-time fans who reveled in his unorthodox skills, he'll never be forgotten.

Chuck Darling

Chuck Darling was a huge success at every step of his basketball career, starting as a high school all-state player in both Montana and Colorado, then becoming an All-Big Ten center and a unanimous All-American at Iowa, and finally making the all-star team all five years he played in the National Industrial Basketball League (NIBL).

If you have never heard of the NIBL, rest assured that it was a big deal when Darling played for the Phillips Oilers back in the middle 1950s. Major corporations such as Phillips

66 of Bartlesville, Oklahoma; Akron's Goodyear Tire and Rubber Company; and the Peoria Caterpillars hired outstanding players to represent their companies in high-level competition. The league rivaled professional basketball in popularity and in salaries that were paid the top players.

When it came time to hold the 1956 Olympic trials, the Phillips Oilers emerged as the winning team, and they would represent the United States in the upcoming Olympics. Darling even outscored and outrebounded the great Bill Russell in the championship showdown game against the College All-Stars. That meant an almost automatic gold medal for Chuck, which

Gone, But Not Retired!

Although Iowa has retired some of the numbers of star players from past years, the school's only two consensus All-Americans didn't need to be accorded that honor. Murray Wier wore number 17 to fame and Chuck Darling number 27, two numbers no longer allowed in basketball.

Many years ago, in an effort to alleviate confusion when an official signals fouls to the scorers' bench, the National Basketball Rules Committee decided to limit uniform numbers to from 0 to 5 or any combination of those digits. An official has an easy time signaling 15 or 23 with the fingers on one hand, for example, but not 17 or 27.

came in due time when the Americans won the Olympic title at Melbourne, Australia, with eight consecutive lopsided victories. They walloped Russia in the championship game, 89–55.

Thus, when you examine Darling's basketball exploits, very little went wrong. And that's why the last game of his illustrious career at Iowa in 1952 sticks out like a bad dream. The Hawkeyes had lost only twice all season, they were playing a so-so Wisconsin team, they were at home, and they still had an outside chance of tying Illinois for the Big Ten title. Not even a blizzard raging outside could keep fans away from the Iowa Fieldhouse. A crowd of more than 11,000 turned out to see the 6'9" Darling cap off his glorious career with an expected routine victory. After all, Wisconsin had won only two conference games all season.

Iowa coach Bucky O'Connor altered his usual starting lineup, which included a brilliant freshman named Deacon Davis, to let five seniors take the floor for the opening tip-off. Maybe that's what threw the Hawks off their normal rhythm, but only Darling seemed up to the task, and he played perhaps his finest game as a collegian, pouring in 34 points and snaring 30 rebounds to set a school record that hasn't been topped in all the intervening years. But the trouble was, many of the rebounds were missed shots by his teammates. Wisconsin pulled off a 78–75 upset victory.

"What a big disappointment that was," says Darling. "To make matters worse, Wisconsin also beat Illinois in the last game that season—so if we had won, we'd have tied Illinois for first place and gotten into a playoff. Instead, Illinois won the title and went to the NCAA tournament, and we had to settle for second place."

Chuck Darling shows the hook shot that carried him to unanimous All-America honors in 1952.

Strangely, Darling played for three different coaches at Iowa because of an unusual set of circumstances. Freshmen weren't eligible to play when he started there, so Chuck had to sit out his first year, 1948–49. That was no hardship for him since he was an honor student majoring in geology. He enjoyed his time in the classroom and formed good study habits, getting a head start on becoming a Phi Beta Kappa scholar. He also spent countless hours jumping rope in the Fieldhouse, working to improve his agility and coordination. "That was good for my conditioning," he said. "We didn't have all the strength training programs they have now. It's really amazing how good the athletes are these days—they're so talented. The players are better, the training is better, and the coaching is better."

O'Connor was the new freshman coach when Chuck arrived, working under the school's successful but highly volatile head coach, Pops Harrison. Before Chuck's sophomore year began, Harrison had major surgery to remove his gall bladder, and although he coached for the first month of the 1949–50 season, he'd been slow in recovering and doctors advised him to take some time off from the rigors of coaching. O'Connor assumed command in January to finish out what was a 15–7 season, with Darling averaging an undistinguished 9.2 points.

Then came a surprise. Athletic Director Paul Brechler had had several run-ins with Harrison over salary matters (Pops wanted more money) and a lack of assistants to help him (one reason O'Connor was hired), and this seemed a convenient time to replace the head coach. Much to Harrison's distress and over his loud complaints, Brechler elevated Rollie Williams from the administrative staff—he had been Harrison's predecessor before

World War II—to coach for the 1950–51 season. It was understood that O'Connor would take over the head job one year later, which was great news for Darling.

"I enjoyed playing for Bucky," says Chuck. "He and I really saw eye to eye. I'll tell you what kind of a person he was. In my freshman year there were a hundred guys out for basketball. Nineteen of us were on scholarship and there was only one spot left—a total of twenty spots. But Bucky treated everyone equally. After two days he knew every kid by name."

Under Rollie Williams in his junior year, Darling led a starting unit of Franklin Calsbeek, Herb Thompson, Bob Clifton, and Ev Cochrane to a 15–7 season and a third-place finish in the Big Ten. Chuck averaged 16.3 points per game and made the all-conference team. Because all the starters except Calsbeek were underclassmen, O'Connor was inheriting an obvious title contender when he took over in the fall of 1951.

The Hawks didn't disappoint—at least not until that final game. Helped by the addition of McKinley "Deacon" Davis, an extremely gifted freshman, they began the season with twelve straight victories before Indiana finally derailed them in Bloomington. Then they won five more in a row, heading into the last two weeks of the season with a 17–1 record. Darling had developed a deadly hook shot with either hand, and he was dominating the league.

Now it was showdown time—a trip to Champaign for a key rematch with Illinois. When they had tangled earlier in Iowa City, Darling picked up four fouls in the first half and then carefully avoided getting any more while sparking the Hawkeyes' 73–68 triumph.

"Unfortunately, I came down with the flu before we played at Illinois," he said. "And then there was a weather problem getting over there. We were supposed to fly over the day before, but the flight was delayed by bad weather. They said the weather would clear the next day, but it didn't, and there was talk of postponing the game. Finally, Illinois said if we would drive over they would keep playing the jayvee game to entertain the crowd until we got there.

"That's what we did. We drove limousines over and we were late getting there. The game didn't start until about eleven o'clock and didn't get over until almost one in the morning. It may have been the only game in Big Ten history to go past midnight."

This was the Illinois team that featured center Johnny "Red" Kerr and an All-America guard in Rod Fletcher. Under the best of conditions, it was going to be a tough game. "We hung with them for a while," says Darling, "but they wound up winning by a pretty big score [78–62]."

MVPs

When Chuck Darling wound up his brilliant career at Iowa as a unanimous All-American in 1952, he was an obvious choice to win the *Chicago Tribune's* Silver Basketball trophy as the most valuable player in the Big Ten. Iowa's only other winners were Murray Wier in 1948 and Sam Williams in 1968.

When his senior season ended, Darling was voted the Big Ten's most valuable player, made every All-America team, and owned almost all the conference scoring records for one year and a career. He totaled 364 points in fourteen conference games (a 26.0 average) to shatter the previous best (277 points). His name remained all over Iowa's school record book for many years. It's still there in some spots. Nobody has come within 5 of matching his 30 rebounds in a game, and his single-season rebounding average of 16.7 as a junior remains the best in Hawkeye history.

Darling was already a promising basketball player by the start of his sophomore year in high school at Helena, Montana, tall for his age at 6'2". Then he began to grow . . . and grow . . . and grow. He grew 6 inches in six months! A promising basketball player was suddenly an all-state player by the end of his sophomore season. Then the family moved to Colorado, and Chuck enrolled at South Denver High School. Can't you just picture the look on the face of the Helena basketball coach when he learned his star player was moving to Colorado?

Helena's loss was South Denver's gain. After big Chuck arrived, South Denver lost the first game of his junior season and the last game in his senior year but won everything in between, including the Colorado state championship when he was a junior. And here is where a bit of luck entered the picture for Iowa. Chuck's father had earned graduate degrees at Iowa, and, in fact, Chuck was born in the western Iowa town of Denison. He'd spent his early years growing up in the Iowa City area. When Hawkeye coach Pops Harrison heard this, and that Chuck was interested in majoring in geological engineering at Iowa, he was on the next plane to Denver. "I'd always been intrigued by rocks and rock formations since my Boy Scout days in Montana," Darling said. "I knew I wanted to get into that kind of work, and Iowa had a good geology program. Actually, it came down to either Iowa or Yale. I never regretted my decision, because I felt Iowa would be better for me." He laughingly added, "My mother never forgave me for not going to Yale."

Seldom if ever did Phillips Petroleum find a potential employee with better qualifications for what the company wanted—a geologist who had been a brain in the classroom and a star on the basketball court. "Through my basketball success, I became acquainted with Lou Wilke of Phillips, who was in the company's sales department in Denver," Darling relates. "That's when I started pointing for a career with Phillips. I saw the Phillips basketball team play quite a few games and was a real fan of Bob Kurland [a 7-footer who preceded Darling with the Oilers]."

He's Still in the Book

Chuck Darling's name is still in the Big Ten record book among the leading single-game rebounders in conference history. The only player to top his 30 rebounds was Indiana's Walt Bellamy with 33 against Michigan in 1961. Paul Morrow of Wisconsin in 1953 and Jerry Lucas of Ohio State in 1962 were others who snared 30 in one conference game.

As he had with the Hawkeyes, Darling set numerous records with Phillips, was twice chosen as the NIBL's most valuable player, and was on the all-star team all five years he played in the league. The highlight of his postgraduate career came on April 4, 1956, when the amateur champion Phillips Oilers squared off against the College All-Stars in Kansas City for the championship of the Olympic trials.

Ironically, the coach of the All-Stars was Darling's old college coach, Bucky O'Connor, who was blessed with having 6'10" giant Bill Russell on his side. Russell had just completed an unbeaten season by helping his San Francisco team beat Iowa's Fabulous Five in the final game of the NCAA tournament. The U.S. Olympic coach would be the man whose team won the trial—either O'Connor or Gerald Tucker of the Oilers. So O'Connor's fate was mostly in the hands of his former star.

In pregame bantering at a coaches luncheon, Tucker had ribbed O'Connor about not letting the All-Stars be too tough on Darling. "Don't kid me, Coach," Bucky replied. "I happen to know what that Darling can do."

O'Connor then proceeded to watch Darling knock him out of the Olympic coaching job with what some observers— including Bucky himself—felt was the finest game of his career. Chuck came through with 21 points and 10 rebounds, 2 points and 3 rebounds better than Russell.

Phillips won the game and the playoffs, 79–75.

"Russell was a great basketball player," Darling says, "but I think there was more physical contact than he was used to. There wasn't much body contact allowed when I played college ball, either. I'm glad I played him when I did. Two or three years later, it might have been a different story." Russell, of course, went on to a great career in pro basketball with the Boston Celtics.

Darling and the other four Phillips starters were automatic selections for the Olympic team. Among the All-Stars chosen along with Russell was Iowa's Carl Cain. Both Darling and Cain were hampered by injuries on the Olympic trip. Darling missed the last two games with a sprained ankle, and Cain was slowed by a painful back injury that turned out to be a herniated disk, effectively ending his career. But they weren't needed. The U.S. team had far too much firepower for the other countries, winning all eight games by at least 30 points.

Since he had to keep himself in tip-top condition for the Olympics, Chuck decided to play one more season in the NIBL, and the results were the same. He wound up his career by leading the Phillips team to its ninth straight league championship. Just as he did at Iowa, he left behind a passel of records before launching a well-traveled business career. During his playing days he had spent one summer in Alaska and another in the Texas Panhandle with oil exploration crews. Later, he was gone for long stretches overseas, including three years in London and four managing the Phillips operations in Egypt.

Darling didn't give up competitive sports when he reached his retirement years. He just switched to a different game, playing in age-group volleyball tournaments around Denver and also competing on the national level with teammates from all over the country in what is known as the Huntsman Cup. Chuck's size, of course, made him just as tough an opponent on the volleyball court as he was in basketball.

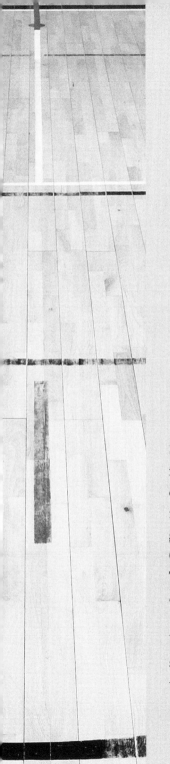

Iowa's Honor Roll

Sam Barry, Ralph Miller, and Lute Olson all followed the same path into the coaches wing of the National Basketball Hall of Fame, winning Big Ten championships at Iowa and then going on to dominant careers in the Pacific Coast Conference, now known as the Pac-10. They accounted for five of the eight conference titles won by the Hawkeyes.

Barry won two in the early days of college basketball, sharing first place in the league standings in 1923 and 1926. From there he went to the University of Southern California and coached teams that topped the old Pacific Coast Conference in 1930, 1935, and 1940. In 1948 Barry guided USC's baseball team to the NCAA championship.

Miller has the unusual distinction of being one of the few coaches to be honored as the coach of the year in three major conferences, not once but twice—first at Wichita State in the Missouri Valley, then at Iowa with Big Ten title teams in 1968 and 1970, and later at Oregon State in the Pac-10. He was the Associated Press national coach of the year in 1981 and 1982.

Olson captured one Big Ten title at Iowa in 1979 and had a surprising Final Four team in 1980 before he began his long and distinguished career at Arizona. He is the modern-day John Wooden in the Pac-10, owning ten conference championships so far and there might be more, because he is still coaching in 2006

A Quadruple Tie

Sam Barry's 1926 Hawkeyes finished in a four-way deadlock for the Big Ten championship with Michigan, Indiana, and Purdue, all posting 8–4 records in conference games. It was the first of only two quadruple title ties in one hundred years of Big Ten basketball. The other was in 2002 when Ohio State, Illinois, Indiana, and Wisconsin all wound up on top at 11–5.

at the age of seventy-one. Olson's teams have averaged nearly twenty-three victories per year in over thirty years of coaching, including one NCAA title at Arizona in 1997. He was the national coach of the year in 1988 and 1990.

Sam Barry

Justin "Sam" Barry was born about the time basketball was invented, in 1892, and grew up in Wisconsin to become a three-sport star—in football, basketball and baseball—at Madison High School. He concentrated on basketball at Lawrence College, captaining the team his senior year, and then coached at Knox College in Galesburg, Illinois, from 1918 to 1922. He spent seven years at Iowa, winning two Big Ten titles and posting a 61–54 record before moving out west to USC.

In addition to his three Pacific Coast championships, Barry's teams won the Southern Division of the conference seven times and finished third in the 1940 NCAA tournament.

Barry was an early advocate of two major rules changes, calling for teams to get the ball across midcourt within 10 seconds, so they would have less time to stall, and elimination of the center jump after every basket. Jump balls obviously slowed things down and the game became much faster and more interesting when this change went into effect in 1937.

Barry's overall basketball coaching record, compiled over a period of twenty-nine years, was 357–211, including 260–138 in his eighteen-year stint at USC.

Ralph Miller

Ralph Miller was a crusty, chain-smoking, self-confident coach who knew the ins and outs of basketball and wanted to make sure that everyone around him knew it. He coached what people liked to see, he said, pressuring opponents with a defensive frenzy that would eventually let his teams win many more games than they lost.

One night when he was the Iowa coach, Miller entertained a group of writers and broadcasters with stories of his successes at previous coaching stops. Large crowds saw his Wichita East High School team win a state title and even larger ones filled the Roundhouse when he led Wichita State to the Missouri Valley championship. It wouldn't be long before the Iowa Fieldhouse would be sold out for every game, too, he boasted. "I'm like a doctor of basketball," said Ralph. "If you have a medical problem, you go to the doctor. If you have a basketball problem, you go to Ralph Miller. I know how to put butts in the seats."

Well, as Dizzy Dean once said, "It ain't bragging if you can do it." And Miller did it. His 1968 Hawkeyes, featuring a one-man point machine in Sam Williams, shared the Big Ten title, and his 1970 team went unbeaten in the conference to claim Iowa's last undisputed championship. That outfit averaged 102.9 points in twenty-five games, powered by the brilliant tandem of John Johnson and Fred Brown.

Miller, a Kansas native, was a quarterback on the University of Kansas football team, ranking among the national leaders in passing as a senior in 1941. But basketball was his game. He'd been an all-stater in high school at Chanute, Kansas, and was a three-time all-conference player at KU, learning the art of pres-

Ralph Miller brought lasting fame to Iowa basketball in the late 1960s.

sure basketball and the fundamentals and strategy of the game from Hall of Fame coach Phog Allen. The idea was to put so much defensive pressure on the opponents that they would run out of gas in the closing minutes.

Lanny Van Eman, a longtime Miller assistant coach, who had played for him at Wichita State, recalled one late-game timeout when Ralph told his players, "Okay, now we've got 'em right where we want 'em." Lanny said he looked up at the clock and "we were five points behind with less than two minutes to go. But Ralph knew the other guys were tired and we did have 'em where we wanted 'em. We won the game."

Miller left Iowa after the 1970 season and went to Oregon State, where he coached for another nineteen years, compiling a 298–156 record. His three Pac-10 titles came in consecutive seasons from 1980–82. At the time of his retirement in 1989, he was the eighth winningest coach in Division I history, owning an overall record of 657–382.

Lute Olson

Robert Luther Olson—basketball fans know him simply as Lute—is a native of the Midwest, growing up in North Dakota and playing his college basketball at Augsburg in Minneapolis, graduating in 1956. He began his coaching career by spending six years at two small high schools in Minnesota. So it was a bit strange that he used the cold Midwest weather as one excuse for leaving what he called his "dream job" at Iowa in 1983 and moving to the sunshine of the Southwest at the University of Arizona, no hotbed of basketball.

Well, it didn't take Lute long to heat things up in Tucson. Arizona's team was 4–20 the season before he arrived. The record improved to 11–17 in his first year, then 21–10 the next, and the

Coach Lute Olson led Iowa to five straight NCAA Tournament appearances.

Wildcats were off and running. They've won ten Pac-10 titles since he's been there.

Olson coached at several California high schools in the Los Angeles area before he became the head coach at Long Beach City College in 1969. A five-year record of 103–20 there earned him the Long Beach State job in 1973, and it was quickly off to Iowa after his team won twenty-four of twenty-six games that season. The Hawkeyes had drifted downhill once Ralph Miller departed, and his successor, Dick Schultz, was fired after four years.

Olson made slow but steady progress, finishing in the Big Ten's first division twice in his first four seasons, then leading an underdog Iowa team to a tie for the conference championship in 1979 and the first of five straight trips to the NCAA tournament. Despite a fourth-place Big Ten finish in 1980, Lute's band of walking wounded survived numerous injuries and made it all the way to the Final Four before they were stopped by Louisville in the semifinals.

A Unique Distinction

When Lute Olson guided Arizona to the 1997 national championship, the Wildcats accomplished an unprecedented feat: They are the only team in NCAA history to beat three number one seeds in the same year.

At the time Olson left Iowa after the 1983 season, he was the winningest coach in school history with a nine-year record of 114–59. His overall totals are staggering—more than 1,000 victories starting with his high school days forty years ago. And now silver-haired Lute has passed the 600-win mark at Arizona. In thirty-three years as a Division I coach, he stands 762–269 for a winning percentage of .750.

Team of the Century:
A Recruiting Windfall

How Herb Wilkinson got to Iowa is a story for the ages. It's almost as if this budding All-American fell out of the trees and right into the lap of Hawkeye coach Pops Harrison.

The way Wilkinson and his youthful University of Utah teammates won the 1944 NCAA championship is an unusual story in itself. They weren't even supposed to be in the tournament. Utah had gone to New York City that year to play in the National Invitational Tournament at Madison Square Garden, a more prestigious honor at the time than competing in the infant NCAA meet. But the Utes lost to Kentucky in the first round and their season was over, or so it seemed.

Then destiny intervened. The University of Arkansas team was in an automobile accident and several key players had been seriously injured, so the Razorbacks were forced to withdraw from the Western Regional of the NCAA tourney. Before leaving New York for the long train ride home, Utah was invited to stop off in Kansas City and join the NCAA field as a replacement for Arkansas.

The Utes didn't waste this opportunity for redemption. They beat Missouri in the first round and emerged number one in the West with a 40–31 victory over Iowa State. Then it was back on the train for a return trip to New York to meet Dartmouth's Eastern Regional champions for the NCAA title.

While all this was going on, Wilkinson's older brother, Clayton, was toiling quietly on a Mormon mission in Cedar Rapids, 25 miles north of Iowa City. Like Herb, Clay also played basketball in his freshman season at Utah. He then left to do two years of church work, and in his free time he began competing in a Cedar Rapids YMCA league. It was soon obvious that Clay was no ordinary "Y" player, and one of Pops Harrison's friends tipped him off that it might be wise to make a short recruiting trip to Cedar Rapids.

Herb Wilkinson picks up the story there: "Pops' friend told him, 'You'd better come up and see this guy—he's good enough to play for you.' So Pops went up, and they talked about Clay going to Iowa. Clay said he wanted to go to dental school, and Pops said Iowa had a good one. And Clay said, 'If I come, I'd like to bring my little brother with me.' Pops said that could probably be arranged, although he didn't know anything about me except that I was in my first year at Utah."

"Little brother" was only a matter of age, by the way. Both Wilkinsons were tall for players of that era, Clay standing 6'5" and Herb 6'4". The same day that Pops met Clay, Utah was playing Dartmouth in Madison Square Garden for the NCAA championship. Herb's last-second basket gave the Utes a thrilling 42–40 victory. "The next day, my picture was in the papers with my teammates raising me on their shoulders and carrying me off the floor," Herb said. "Pops right away called Clay and said, 'Is that your little brother?' Clay said yes, and Pops said, 'Hell, bring him along.'"

Utah's rousing finish didn't end there. During the 1943–44 season, the United States was in the midst of World War II. The Red Cross matched the NCAA championship team against the winner of the NIT in a benefit game to aid the armed forces. And the Utes won that one, too. They gained a full measure of revenge for their earlier NIT loss in Madison Square Garden by whipping St. John's, 43–36, to become the champion of champions.

That next fall, Iowa had a benefit of its own, when it added the talented Wilkinson brothers to its basketball roster. They joined incoming freshman Murray Wier and three outstanding rookies from the year before—Dick Ives, Jack Spencer, and Dave Danner—to make up the key elements of the 1945 Big Ten championship team.

"I wanted to go to dental school, too, and postponed my mission to do that," Herb recalls. "Utah didn't have a dental school, and I'd been considering one in Kansas City, but I went to Iowa instead. Can you imagine a recruiting story like that today? Two brothers coming in that way with three years of eligibility. It would never happen.

"We were good enough to win the Big Ten title all three years," he continued. "It's kind of sickening that we didn't. But Clay had to have an operation—he'd fallen on his tailbone one year—and Danner had some back problems. Still, we were good enough to win the championship more than just that first year."

Herb is the only Iowa basketball player in history to be named to the All-Big Ten first team three straight years, earning

All-America recognition all three years as well. He was an easy pick for Iowa's All-Century team. After graduation he decided against playing pro basketball, spending one year in an anesthesiology program, but he then found an offer from the Minneapolis Lakers too appealing to turn down. The Lakers and George Mikan were in their heyday at the time, and Herb agreed to join them, the only stipulation being that he wouldn't play on Sundays.

"One Sunday game I wasn't there and the owner asked where I was," Herb related. "The coach said he doesn't play on Sundays, and the owner sent me a note saying I had to play on Sundays or he would release me. I'm not sure he was serious, but I quit basketball and went off on a mission for two years."

The Lone Survivor

How many basketball teams could survive being shorn of four starters in the middle of a season and still remain in the nation's top ten? Very few, no doubt. But that's what Iowa did in the month of February 1961, when guards Dave Maher and Ron Zagar, center Frank Allen, and forward Tom Harris went to the sidelines because of academic ineligibility.

Junior Don Nelson was the lone survivor on a rugged first five that had been ranked number one in the country just a few weeks earlier, after posting three straight victories on the West Coast to win a holiday tournament. Nelson was the best of the bunch, to be sure, but this was putting an almost hopeless burden on his shoulders.

An Omen: 76-76

After Iowa beat California, 83-80, in a four-overtime game at the Los Angeles Classic in 1960, famed Iowa native Meredith Willson went to the dressing room and asked to speak to the Hawkeyes. Willson wrote the songs and lyrics to *The Music Man*, including the hit tune "76 Trombones." He congratulated the players, then quipped, "When the score was 76-76 I knew you had 'em."

The Hawks were still among the nation's elite teams, holding down the number nine position with a 12–3 record, when their coach, Sharm Scheuerman, went to work trying to reconstruct a new starting lineup. An upcoming road trip to always-strong Indiana added to the grim outlook. Wisconsin would come after that, to be immediately followed by Ohio State's defending national champions, the current number one team. "Fortunately, we had a good group of guys," Scheuerman remembered. "The reserves weren't as good as the starters, of course, but we were still pretty good."

Football quarterback Matt Szykowny, a strong all-around athlete, proved to be a valuable replacement in a new front line with 6'9" Dennis Runge and the 6'6" Nelson. Joel Novak, Nelson's former high school teammate at Rock Island, and Joe Reddington took over at the two guard spots. And Dick Shaw, a 6'7" sophomore, assumed more of a presence as the new sixth man. "I felt more responsibility, and my teammates expected me to carry a

Don Nelson was the glue that held Iowa's 1960–61 top-ten team together.

bigger portion of the load," said Nelson. "I still look back on that as one of the highlights of my whole career. Sharm did a terrific job of coaching, and we played some terrific basketball."

The embattled Hawks righted themselves and won six of their last nine games, starting with a completely unexpected 74–67 victory at Indiana. Wisconsin then fell, 63–61, and that set the stage for one of the most memorable games ever played in Iowa Fieldhouse. Ohio State came in boasting the likes of All-America Jerry Lucas, along with John Havlicek and Larry Siegfried from their NCAA title team of the year before.

It would be nice to put a happy ending to this story—and there could just as well have been one. Iowa led almost all the way, and by 59–52 in the late stages, but the Buckeyes rallied to escape, 62–61, when Nelson missed a short turnaround jumper from the lane with time running out. "And Dick Shaw just missed tipping in that shot," said Nelson. Scheuerman didn't see how the tip could not have gone down, saying, "It did a complete 360 around the rim."

The box score shows that Nelson and Lucas fought to a standoff, each scoring 25 points, but it also shows how valiantly the Hawks had fought. They outrebounded Ohio State by a whopping 35–23.

Something happened with 2:20 left that may have helped determine the outcome, although no one on the Iowa bench complained at the time. Iowa was leading, 58–55, when Szykowny fouled Ohio State's Gary Gearhart. But instead of Gearhart going to the line, Siegfried—an 88 percent free thrower—got away with an old bit of trickery. He stepped up as though he'd been fouled and made both attempts.

The Hawks finished their topsy-turvy season with an 18–6 record, going 10–4 to tie for second place in the Big Ten. Nelson averaged 23.7 and, of course, was voted their most valuable player. When he wound up his career in 1962, he'd been the leading scorer, top rebounder, and team MVP three straight years. He was also All-Big Ten both as a junior and senior.

A long and almost unparalleled career followed in pro basketball. Nelson spent many years playing for the Boston Celtics, became a prominent NBA coach for several teams, compiling well over 1,100 victories, and then rose to the general manager's post with the Dallas Mavericks. He and Pat Riley are the only NBA coaches to be named coach of the year three times.

Among the Others

Iowa's twenty-man All-Century team was chosen by a vote of fans and by a panel of veteran personnel from the university's athletic department. At the time it was released in 2002, two former stars were deceased—Ben Selzer, who earned All-America recognition in 1934, and Dick Ives, a high-scoring All-American and four-year letterman in the 1940s.

Dave Gunther was the scoring leader and MVP three years in a row, playing on Bucky O'Connor's last two teams in 1957–58, and then for Sharm Scheuerman as a senior. Seven-foot Kevin Kunnert had to carry the load on three second-division teams, but he was accorded All-America honors as a senior in 1973, setting a school career rebounding record that lasted over thirty years until Greg Brunner surpassed it in 2006.

Team of the Century

B. J. Armstrong, Team MVP, 1988, 1989

Fred Brown, All-American, 1971

Carl Cain, Team MVP, 1954–56

Chuck Darling, Consensus All-American, 1952

Acie Earl, 1992 Big Ten defensive player of year

Dave Gunther, Team MVP, 1957–59

Dick Ives, Top scorer, 1944–46

John Johnson, 699 points, 1970

Kevin Kunnert, Team MVP, 1972, 1973

Ronnie Lester, Team MVP, 1978–80

Bill Logan, Top scorer, 1954–56

Roy Marble, Top career scorer, 2,116 points

Don Nelson, Team MVP, 1960–62

Bill Seaberg, Star guard for the "Fabulous Five"

Ben Selzer, All-America mention, 1934

Greg Stokes, Top scorer, 1983–85

Murray Wier, Consensus All-American, 1948

Herb Wilkinson, All–Big Ten, 1945–47

Sam Williams, Big Ten MVP, 1968

Andre Woolridge, Led Big Ten, points and assists, 1996

The Fabulous Five

One day in late 1952, when Bucky O'Connor was early in his second season as Iowa's head basketball coach, he told his young assistant, Bob Schulz, to send in some players from the freshman team to scrimmage against the varsity, with one important stipulation from past requests: "Mix them up, Bob," said O'Connor. "Don't send in those same five guys. They're killing us."

The five freshmen who had been embarrassing their veteran counterparts in practice sessions formed one of the greatest teams in the annals of Hawkeye basketball: Bill Logan, Carl Cain, Bill Seaberg, Sharm Scheuerman, and Bill Schoof. After they ended their careers four years later one game shy of winning the national championship, all five of their numbers were retired.

Freshman eligibility was a hotly debated topic back then. Except for wartime emergencies, incoming freshmen had to sit out a year to work on their studies before moving up to varsity play. The rule had been relaxed for the 1951–52 season because of the Korean War, which was why Deacon Davis became an immediate starter for the Hawks in his rookie year, but the rule makers changed it back after that one year. So the players who would eventually be known as the Fabulous Five had to cool their heels and beat up on the varsity whenever they could.

The Sensational Six?

Hugh Leffingwell, an all-state player from Marion, showed great promise when he joined Bucky O'Connor's standout recruiting class of 1952, the group that produced the Fabulous Five. But Leffingwell died of leukemia before he got a chance to play much. "People tend to forget just how good he was," said Bob Schulz, who coached the rookies in 1952–53. "If Hugh had lived, we might have had the Sensational Six, not just the Fabulous Five."

The Fabulous Five with coach Bucky O'Connor, from left: Sharm Scheuerman, Bill Logan, Carl Cain, Bill Schoof, and Bill Seaberg.

O'Connor was forced to begin a major reconstruction job in 1952 after the loss of his All-American, Chuck Darling. The Hawks limped home with a 9–9 record in the 1953 Big Ten standings, slipping to a sixth-place finish, but then the rookies took over. Logan, a 6'6" former all-state player from Keokuk, was the only native Iowan of the bunch. All the others were from Illinois, discards that their home-state university didn't want. Logan, Cain, and Seaberg quickly became starters as sophomores, along with Davis and another holdover, Chuck Jarnagin. This was a potent outfit, too, especially with the likes of Scheuerman and Shoof coming off the bench, and by mid-February 1954, they had won nine of their first ten conference games.

But then the alarm signals went off. Maybe these guys really weren't as good as they were cracked up to be, because after losing a road game at Ohio State, they returned to Iowa City, where Illinois pulverized them, 74–51. That one sent fans streaming for the exits long before the game was over. And to make matters worse for O'Connor and his disillusioned youngsters, two days after the Illinois debacle, they had to be in Bloomington to face Indiana's defending national champions. The Hoosiers, 10–1 and on their way to a second straight conference title, featured the likes of 6'10" Don Schlundt and All-America guard Bob Leonard.

What to do? O'Connor wrestled with that question all weekend. Or was there anything he could do? In desperation he decided to bench his two upperclassmen, Jarnagin and Davis, and start an all-sophomore lineup of Scheuerman and Schoof with Seaberg, Logan, and Cain.

"We went through our normal pregame warmup," recalled Seaberg, "and when we got back to the dressing room Bucky said he was going to change the lineup. He said Sharm and Schoof would start with Logan, Cain, and myself. Well, that surprised us all—five sophomores starting together for the first time. It really fired us up. Remember, that was a great Indiana team we were facing, with almost everybody back from the national champions of the year before. I'm sure they didn't expect much from us. We were pretty much an unknown team but we really had the intensity that night.

"My job was to guard Leonard, and Bucky said, 'Don't let that Leonard get away from you.' I think I chased him all the way into the dressing room at halftime."

Meanwhile, the news that he would start at the guard spot opposite Seaberg hit Scheuerman almost like a kick in the stomach—literally. "I got sick," Sharm said. "After I threw up, I told our trainer, Doyle Allsup, 'Don't tell Bucky, don't tell Bucky.' I was afraid he wouldn't let me play. Doyle took a bucket out to the bench, and I had to use it a couple more times. I thought it was just a case of nerves, and that was probably part of it, but actually I was coming down with the flu and had to be hospitalized when we got home."

It was an otherwise happy homecoming, though, because the young Hawks had given a clear indication of what was ahead by upsetting the Hoosiers, 82–64. Iowa then beat Michigan State and Ohio State to finish a satisfying 17–5 season, and the 11–3 conference showing was good enough for a second place behind Indiana (12–2).

The next two years were among the most memorable in Hawkeye history with back-to-back Big Ten championships, and there might have been a national title as well if it hadn't been for one gigantic obstacle, the brilliant Bill Russell of San Francisco. Iowa made it to the Final Four in both 1955 and 1956, losing to LaSalle in the semifinals the first time, then falling victim to the defensive mastery of Russell the following year in the championship game. Russell was an agile shot-blocking whiz, and he also had the advantage of not having to worry about being called for goaltending. There was no rule against goaltending back then.

"That made a whale of a difference for him," said Logan. "He caused a change in the rules the next year or the year after. The change was called the 'Russell Rule'—you couldn't block a shot on its downward path. He was credited with 27 rebounds in our game, and it's still an NCAA tournament record, but I think a lot of those were blocked shots."

Iowa had won the last fourteen games of the regular season to win the Big Ten title, then three more in tourney play to reach the 1956 NCAA final. But that seventeen-game streak was puny compared with what Russell and San Francisco were doing. When the Dons captured the 1955 national championship, they finished with twenty-six straight victories, and they were riding a fifty-four-game winning streak the next year when they took Iowa to the woodshed, 83–71.

"I remember we got off to a 14–4 lead and Russell called time out," said Logan. "I think he decided it was time for him to take off the warmups, because when he came back, he was all business. It was a new game after that. None of us had ever seen anything like him."

In addition to patrolling the backboards and swatting away so many of Iowa's shot attempts, Russell led all scorers with 26 points. Afterward, O'Connor sympathized with what his players had been up against, saying, "It's tough to have the ball batted back at you time after time." Logan noted that "you can jump as high as you can and still you're only high enough to tap Russell on the shoulder."

After the sophomore-dominated lineup had made such a strong finish in 1954, it was only natural that the Hawkeyes would be solid favorites to win the Big Ten title in 1955. And they did, with the same 11–3 record of the year before being good enough to claim first place, helped by a crucial 72–70 late-season victory at the University of Minnesota before a then-record collegiate crowd of 20,176. Five Hawks played the whole game—Scheuerman, who hit the winning basket, with Seaberg, Logan, Davis, and Cain. Davis was a senior that season and started most of the time ahead of Schoof, so the "Fabulous Five" nickname was still a year away.

Iowa's trip to the Final Four in Kansas City, where LaSalle would be the semifinal opponent, was not looked upon with great anticipation by the two African Americans on the squad, Davis and Cain, because they were well aware that Missouri could be hostile territory for blacks. Basketball teams of that era were mostly all white, although San Francisco was coming in with two African-American standouts, Russell and K. C. Jones.

"All the teams were staying at the Muehlebach Hotel, and we became friendly with players on the other teams," Cain recalled. "One night a bunch of us went out to dinner together—blacks and whites together—and we got stopped at the door of the restaurant. The black guys were told that we had to go to the back door. And Russell said, 'The back door? What, do we get a discount or something?' We got a laugh out of that, but the message was clear. We left together and went someplace else."

LaSalle had an outstanding player in Tom Gola, and he proved to be the difference as the Hawks lost their semifinal game, 76–73. They made a poor showing in the third-place game and lost that one, too, bowing to Colorado, 75–54. Russell and San Francisco easily disposed of LaSalle in the championship final, 77–63.

Slow Change

First it was Deacon Davis who was shunned in his home state, by the University of Illinois. The next year Carl Cain got the same treatment—meaning no interest at all. Both were from Freeport in northern Illinois, both were star basketball players in high school, and both were African American. "It was rather obvious that Illinois didn't want any black players back in the early 1950s," Cain says. "We went to Champaign and won the state championship when Deacon was a senior and I was a junior, and my team went back to the Sweet Sixteen the next year, so it wasn't like they didn't know who we were."

After being snubbed by his home-state school University of Illinois, Deacon Davis went on to become a star for the Hawkeyes.

Not that Davis and Cain would have gone to Illinois, but it was the purposeful snub that hurt. Iowa Coach Bucky O'Connor took full advantage of the situation in what was almost a package deal.

"Deacon was my next-door neighbor, and he asked me to drive over with him to see the campus in Iowa City," Cain explained. "He said he planned to go there, and when we were leaving to come home, Bucky told me, 'Now, Carl, when it comes time for you to go to college, I hope you'll consider Iowa.' That really impressed me."

Davis was a four-year starter for the Hawkeyes (freshmen were eligible his first year, 1951–52), and Cain was a three-year starter on the Fabulous Five that went to the Final Four in both 1955 and 1956. Unfortunately for Iowa, that was the era of two-time champion San Francisco and legendary Bill Russell.

About that time the racial landscape began gradually changing. Nolden Gentry, now a Des Moines attorney, was one of the first African-American players invited for a visit to Illinois after he'd led his Rockford West team to state championships in both 1955 and 1956. Illinois Coach Harry Combes sent a plane especially to bring Gentry and one of his African-American teammates in for a visit. "At the all-state banquet my senior year," Gentry said, "Harry Combes almost had tears in his eyes when he said: 'I'm getting sick and tired of seeing all these Illinois kids go over to Iowa and come back to beat us.'"

But where Gentry was concerned, the plea fell on deaf ears. He followed Davis and Cain to Iowa and became a three-year starter in 1958–60. By that time African Americans were playing at Illinois and earning spots on teams all over the country.

The 1956 season that made the Fabulous Five famous began in almost total disaster. In late November Scheuerman got kicked in the kidney playing touch football and was hospitalized for several weeks. He couldn't play much in December, and a trip to the West Coast resulted in three straight losses—close ones to Washington and Stanford and then a 70–45 thrashing by California. The Hawks hardly looked like the team that was supposed to win the Big Ten.

Wait, it gets worse. They came home and promptly lost their Big Ten opener to Michigan State, 65–64, which was all the more galling because they'd built a 60–47 lead and then blew it in the last seven minutes. O'Connor would need a miraculous turnaround to salvage the season. "I remember a headline in the *Des Moines Register* saying we had 'senioritis,' and I think that kind of woke us up," Logan said. "We had a meeting over at Bucky's house one night, but he didn't chew us out or anything. It was just a general discussion and everybody entered into it, talking about the things we needed to do."

Next up was a trip to Ohio State to face one of the Big Ten's all-time deadeyes, Robin Freeman, the nation's second leading scorer that year, averaging 32 points per game. Scheuerman was given the unenviable task of trying to guard him. "When we came in at halftime, Freeman had something like 27 points," Logan related. "Bucky said, 'You're doing a nice job, Sharm, keep it up.' We kind of chuckled about that, but Bucky didn't change anything. Freeman finished with 37, but that was okay, because we knew one player wouldn't beat us."

Iowa won by the healthy margin of 88–73, beginning the long winning streak that didn't end until the run-in with Bill Russell. Home or away, it made no difference to the Fabulous Five. Those Hawkeyes actually won slightly more games on foreign courts in the Big Ten than they did at home, a rather startling statistic considering how tough it is for teams to win on the road. In three seasons, 1954–56, Iowa's road record in conference games was 18–3, compared to 17–4 at home.

To a man, the five will tell you there is one game that stands out above all the others in their book of fond memories—the 96–72 rout of Illinois to clinch the 1956 Big Ten championship. Both teams were 11–1 atop the conference race when they met for the only time that season, squaring off in a Saturday afternoon game at the Fieldhouse on regional television. The stakes were much higher then than they would be now as far as the NCAA tournament was concerned, since only the Big Ten champion advanced to the sixteen-team field back then. This was a showdown for that coveted spot.

Scheuerman remembers looking out his Hillcrest dormitory window and seeing students noisily climbing up the Grand Avenue Hill toward the Fieldhouse—at 8:30 in the morning! The game wasn't scheduled to start until 1:30. "I was told they caused such a ruckus outside that the gates had to be opened early to let them in," said Sharm.

"My wife's ride to the game was late picking her up," recalled Schoof, "and she was worried about getting caught in traffic. Instead, they drove right up to the Fieldhouse, and she got out and walked right in. This was half an hour before the game, and everybody was already there."

Cain says his memory is foggy on most games of yesteryear, "but I'll never forget that one. We just blew 'em away."

It took a while, though. Illinois had such players as big George BonSalle, little Bill Ridley, the Judson twins, Bruce Brothers, and Harv Schmidt. Most had been first-team, all-state players. The joke at the time was that the game matched the Illinois first all-state team against the second and third teams.

Anyway, the atmosphere in the Fieldhouse was charged with enough electricity to light the whole campus as tip-off time approached. Throughout a hard-fought first half, there was little to choose between the two powerhouses, and Iowa went to the halftime break owning a 37–35 lead. But the second half was total annihilation. The Hawks became almost unstoppable, rolling up 59 points. "It was one of those times when we got into a zone and reached a higher level," Logan said. "Something happened, I don't know what it was, but all of a sudden everything we did was right."

Quite simply, said Schoof, "it was the best half of basketball we ever played."

Logan said he personally reached that zone only one other time, scoring a career-high 36 points in Iowa's 83–76 victory over Temple in the 1956 NCAA semifinals—the only Hawkeye victory ever in a Final Four. He needed to be at his best, too, because Temple's hot-shooting guards, Hal Lear and Guy Rodgers, combined to total 60 points. But the Owls obviously had little firepower to go with them. "That was one of those nights when everything went right for me," said Bill. "It was as good as I ever played."

So what made the Fabulous Five tick? Why did they mesh so well together? They weren't a particularly tall team. They were all good athletes, but only Cain would have to be placed in the

A Matter of Faith

Before the players on Iowa's Fabulous Five began their sophomore season, Coach Bucky O'Connor passed out a mimeographed sheet of general instructions and gave his personal philosophy on life. In it he said of religion: "The boy who has faith in God can look to the future without worry or strain. I firmly believe that the boys on our team who attend church are more likely to be successful because they can face their problems with hope and encouragement. Religion plays an important part in the mental attitude of the athlete."

That was it. He never made an issue of the subject, only to say when their playing days were over how pleased he was that they were regular churchgoers.

exceptional category. "I think you could start with the fact that we were a close group, both on and off the court," Seaberg explained. "We enjoyed hanging out together, and we had great respect for one another. Maybe I'd get 20 points in one game, then Logan might get 20 the next, and Cain was always there scoring and sweeping the boards. We all knew our roles."

Cain puts it this way: "My personal assessment is that we were a group of players that had no extraordinary talent. But we came together at Iowa at a time when our skills meshed with the coaching we received. When that happened, we became something special."

Logan agreed. "I think we just complemented each other—Carl's speed, Seaberg's shot from the outside, my shot inside, and Sharm feeding the middle. Sharm's passing into the post was some of the best you'll ever see. And Schoof didn't get the credit he deserved. He was so important in everything we did."

Others are deserving of more recognition, too, according to Schoof. "What gets lost in all the adulation for the Fabulous Five are guys like Babe Hawthorne, Bob George, and Augie Martel—the guys we had on the bench," he said. "They were all good ball players who would have started on almost any other team. They've been almost totally ignored."

The 1956 regular season didn't end with the Illinois victory. For Iowa to clinch an undisputed title, the Hawks still had to dispose of Indiana at home the following Monday night, and while O'Connor feared a possible letdown, the five seniors had come too far to let that happen. They finished with a 13–1 record in conference play by putting the Hoosiers away, 84–73. Afterward, Hoosier star Wallie Choice commented that the Hawkeyes "play better together than any team I've ever seen. Their passing is simply bewildering."

Unbelievably, that same night Illinois was the victim of one of the most shocking upsets in Big Ten history. The Illini, obviously distraught by what had happened in Iowa City, went to Northwestern and lost to a team that hadn't won a conference game all winter. The Wildcats rose up from the ashes of a 0–13 season to knock off Illinois, 81–80.

Coach Bucky O'Connor led Iowa's Fabulous Five to back-to-back Big Ten championships and NCAA Final Four appearances.

Iowa's path to the Final Four in Evanston was made to order—two regional games in the Iowa Fieldhouse, where the Hawks disposed of Morehead State and Kentucky, sending them off to join Temple, San Francisco, and Southern Methodist for the climactic games. The semifinal victory over Temple was an interesting study in contrasts. The Hawkeye front line of Logan (36 points), Cain (20), and Schoof (18) accounted for all but nine of the team's points, while the guard court of Hal Lear (32) and Guy Rodgers (28) carried most of the scoring load for Temple.

When the season came to a close and the statistics were added up, they showed just what kind of team the Fabulous Five had been. All five players averaged in double figures, led by Logan's 17.7 points per game. Cain was next at 15.8, followed by Seaberg 13.9, Schoof 10.8 and Scheuerman 10.1. O'Connor knew it would be a long time before Iowa saw their likes again, saying, "I could coach another fifty years and never have a team—I mean a real everybody-for-everybody unit—like this. It was a coach's dream team."

The players obviously had great respect and affection for their genial coach and were stunned to learn of his death in April 1958, especially Scheuerman, who by that time was Iowa's freshman coach and Bucky's chief assistant. "He had a noon speaking engagement in Waterloo," said Sharm, "and I remember he was running late when he left me off at the golf course that morning. I played nine holes and then walked over to the Quadrangle grill for some ice cream. Somebody came in and said he'd just heard the news on the radio that Bucky had been killed in an automobile accident. I just sat there. I couldn't believe it."

O'Connor apparently had swerved in an effort to miss hitting some guinea hens crossing the two-lane highway southeast of Waterloo, crashing head-on into a truck carrying heavy metal pipes. He was killed instantly. Several weeks later, at age twenty-four, Scheuerman was named to replace him, becoming one of the youngest head coaches in Division I history.

Miller's Dynamic Duo

In the fall of 1969 somebody in the Iowa athletic department had the foresight to order the installation of new basketball scoreboards on the east wall and the balcony overhangs of the Fieldhouse. These added an extra digit to the team totals for scores that reached more than 100 points. What excellent timing!

Coach Ralph Miller's Hawkeyes, powered by the talented twosome of John Johnson and Freddie Brown, were about to take off on an unmatched season in Big Ten history. They soared over the 100-point mark fourteen times in twenty-five games, averaging 102.9 points and 39.9 field goals in conference games. Those are league records that have never been equaled—nor are they likely to be any time soon.

The odd thing is, Miller had come to Iowa from Wichita State five years earlier as a coach who emphasized pressure defense. Run, run, run, and then run some more; tire your opponent out; steal the ball; break the other team's will; and the game will be yours in the closing minutes, if not before that. This was his basic strategy. Scoring points was important to Ralph, of course, but not as much as constant defensive pressure.

But the arrival of the free-wheeling, 6'7" Johnson from a junior college for the 1968–69 season, followed by the 6'3" Brown from another junior college the next year, forced Miller to alter his thinking. They formed a starting unit with two veteran seniors from Pennsylvania, guard Chad Calabria and forward Glenn Vidnovic, and 6'8" junior center Dick Jensen. Jensen didn't score much, but he was a horse on the backboards. Ben McGilmer added an invaluable presence as a forward-center reserve and gave the players their nickname—the "Six Pack."

"Ralph tried to work Johnson and Brown into a certain structure to suit his old philosophy and it didn't work," said Bob Brooks, a longtime Hawkeye broadcaster. "Those guys were street ball players. You couldn't put a harness on them. Once Ralph turned them loose after the first of the year, there was no stopping them."

Freddie Brown helped usher in an era of high scoring for the Hawkeyes.

The December games in the 1969–70 season didn't give much of a hint that extraordinary times were ahead. The Hawks lost four of their first seven games, and the high hopes that came with the arrival of Brown's long-range shooting seemed to be dashed before the conference schedule began. And the first Big Ten opponent in Iowa City was title favorite Purdue, which boasted a brilliant shooter in Rick Mount. That early January matchup was a dandy, with Mount lighting up the Hawks for 53 points, but Johnson and Brown led a more balanced attack that let Iowa prevail, 94–88.

The next two games, which were on the road, proved to the doubters that these players were going to be something special. The Hawkeyes shot a school-record 63.4 percent to outscore Michigan, 107–99, with J. J. pouring in 34 points, Calabria 24, Brown 23, and Vidnovic 18. Then came a trip to Wisconsin that produced a flamboyant highlight reel of fancy play, especially in the first half when Iowa piled up an overwhelming 51–22 lead. Later, when he wrote his autobiography, *Spanning the Years*, Miller called that "the best half any team of mine ever played on the road."

After that 92–74 victory, the Hawks were off to the races in what would be a perfect 14–0 conference season, breaking one record after another—18 school records in all, some of which still stand. When they made it thirteen straight with a 116–97 triumph at Northwestern, Johnson was at his absolute best with a 49-point barrage, which remains as the top individual performance in the annals of Hawkeye basketball. J. J.'s scoring line showed 20 baskets in 23 attempts, plus 9 of 10 from the free throw line.

Raise the Baskets?

Ralph Miller long advocated raising the baskets to 12 feet in college and professional basketball, while keeping them at 10 feet for high schools and below. He loved to argue about this. Many rule changes over the years were designed to limit the advantage of the big man, he said, but the easiest solution was continually overlooked.

The average individual's height back in the days when James Naismith invented the game was about 5'6" or so. Now players much taller than that dominate the game and most 6-footers can easily dunk the ball. There is no beauty in that, Miller claimed. He called the dunk shot an "idiot's delight." Experimental games have proven the validity of higher baskets, Miller said, especially that there would be no dropoff in shooting accuracy, and that they would unclog the lane because of deeper rebounds, but he found little support for such a revolutionary change.

The classic game was yet to come, a late-February rematch with Purdue and Mount in West Lafayette. Iowa was 11–0 in conference play with three games left, and Purdue was the only serious challenger at 9–2. What happened was perhaps the weirdest and wildest of all the basketball games ever played in the Big Ten. For one thing, Mount scored what is still the all-time conference record, 61 points, and yet Purdue could not win the game. Iowa rallied in the closing minutes to pull out a 108–107 thriller. "That was a great college basketball game," said Calabria. "Mount was something else. The three-point shot wasn't in vogue back then, but if it had been, he might have had one hundred points."

Actually, it would have been eighty-three. Years later somebody broke down the film of that game, charted where Mount's shots were launched from, and arrived at that figure, which meant 22 of his 27 baskets (that's still a league record, too) were taken beyond the three-point stripe. "Mount was one of the greatest pure shooters who ever stepped on a court," marveled Miller. "He had 40-foot range and 35 was a snap. Everything else was like a layup. He was the only one-handed shooter I've ever seen with that kind of range."

Before the game there was indecision about who would guard Mount. Finally Brown agreed to tackle the assignment, and later, of course, he took a ribbing for what transpired. "We used to tease Fred that he was just watching Mount out there," said Johnson, but Brown counters, "Our scouting report had J. J., Vidnovic, or Calabria to guard Mount. None of those guys wanted to guard him, so I volunteered. Every time J. J. brings it up, I tell him, remember who got you here, we won the game."

Mount kept firing his long shots, but he suddenly went cold in the final minutes, with Purdue leading, 101–92, and it was Brown's scoring that sparked the Iowa comeback. The game was so hectic that at one point a technical foul was called on Purdue's crowd, after the referees had warned the fans to stop littering the floor. Any more debris, they said, would result in a technical foul and an Iowa free throw.

"There were several more possessions," recalled Brooks, who was broadcasting the game, "and then down came a paper airplane—somebody said later from an Iowa fan. Whoever made it made a perfect one. It circled the court and as soon as it hit the floor, the referee called the technical. He was just waiting for that. I don't remember whether it was then or later, but along in there somewhere the Purdue coach [George King] got so mad he ran out of Mackey Arena. That's how wild it was—the most exciting game I ever saw."

Two more games remained to complete the unblemished conference season, but they were mere formalities for these high-scoring Hawks. When they closed with a 113–92 romp over Ohio State at home and a 115–101 breeze at Northwestern, they had whizzed past the century mark six times in their last eight starts.

Their season averages showed what a perfect blend they'd been with five players scoring in double figures, topped by Johnson's 27.9 school record. Calabria was next at 19.1, Brown 17.4, the rail-thin Vidnovic (at 6'6" the players called him "Stick") 15.7, and McGilmer coming off the bench to contribute 10.3.

"We'd had a poor season the year before," Calabria said, "and in looking back to our success in 1970, you'd have to say Fred Brown was the missing piece to our puzzle. He fit in perfectly.

There were no big egos. We just learned to play well as a team."

As for Brown, he said he knew what his role was, and it wasn't to score a lot of points. "I just filled a need. Those other guys had all been there. I could pass well, and the other guys wanted to shoot. Because I was the point guard, I had the ball. So I got it to them."

Iowa entered the sixteen-team NCAA field that year as an obvious threat to win the national championship, but the first-round opponent in Columbus, Ohio, was Jacksonville State with a dangerously tall lineup that boasted 7'0" Artis Gilmore and 7'1" Pembroke Burrows playing in a double post. Iowa's scouting report said Burrows was a poor shooter, so Miller said his strategy was to sag off and guard Gilmore. Wrong! Burrows made 11 of his 12 shot attempts.

Even after Gilmore fouled out with eight minutes to play, the Hawks could not put the pesky Florida team away. Finally, a basket by Brown with 18 seconds left let Iowa move ahead, 103–102. That seemed to do it. Jacksonville's Vaughn Wedeking missed a desperation 30-footer just before time expired, but the ball bounced high to Burrows for a tip-in that sent the Hawks down to defeat, 104–103. "The ball went over my head, right to Burrows," Calabria said. "And when a guy is as tall as that with such long arms, there wasn't much I could do about it. It wasn't a good feeling when I saw that shot go in."

Those were the days when they still played regional consolation games, so the Hawks had one more game left—against Notre Dame, which had lost in the first round to Kentucky. And Miller made sure his dejected troops were not going to end their great season on a sour note. As it turned out, Notre Dame coach

Johnny Dee offered up all the ammunition Ralph needed in a pregame quote. Asked about playing Iowa, Dee said, "Well, Iowa's got a pretty good ball club, but we've played three or four Big Ten teams and we've beaten them all."

Miller said he didn't appreciate that comment, and "I told our team, 'I want you to do me a favor and take care of Johnny a little bit.'"

According to Calabria, there was a little more to it than that. "Ralph was really emotional before the game," said Chad. "I had never seen him that way. Maybe he knew he was leaving [to take the Oregon State job], I don't know, but I think he wanted us to prove that the Jacksonville loss was a fluke."

So it was time for the Hawks to put on another clinic. After just thirteen minutes Iowa was on top, 53–32. Dee called three timeouts in an effort to stem the tide, but there was no stopping the onslaught. The lead grew to an eye-popping 75–42 at the half. "I almost felt sorry for Johnny Dee at halftime—but not too much," Miller said.

The Hawks eased up in the second half and won easily, 121–106, to set an NCAA tournament scoring record that stood for nineteen years. Calabria pumped in 15 of 22 shots and hit 31 points. J. J. also totaled 31, and Vidnovic had 24.

In reflecting on his long career after retiring at Oregon State, Miller ranked both Johnson and Brown among the top five shooters he ever coached. And he said Brown might have been a better passer than he was a shooter. "That 1970 Iowa group was probably the best all-around team I ever had," he concluded.

Johnson and Brown both were first-round draft choices and enjoyed long pro careers. J. J. spent twelve years with four different

NBA teams, winding up in Seattle, where he joined his old team-mate. Brown was known as "Downtown Freddie" Brown by then because of his long-range accuracy after being shifted from point guard to shooting guard. He was in the pro ranks for thirteen years.

One of Miller's most notable victories at Iowa occurred in his first season, 1964–65, when the underdog Hawks met UCLA in Chicago Stadium and upset Coach John Wooden's defending national champions, 87–82. The stunning form reversal was only the second defeat in forty-five games for a UCLA team ranked number one in the country. Iowa hadn't figured to make it much of a contest with an unimposing 9–5 record.

Jim Zabel, a longtime voice of the Hawkeyes, remembers climbing aboard the team bus after the game and congratulating Miller, saying, "Ralph, how did you do it?" And Miller, puffing on his ever-present cigarette, said, "Easy. The players did exactly what I told them to do."

Overconfidence on UCLA's part might have had something to do with it, too, because the Hawkeyes were mostly an unknown quantity. They had struggled to an 8–15 record the year before, after which Sharm Scheuerman was released as the coach and replaced by Miller from Wichita State.

Miller knew he needed some immediate scoring help, and that's when he began his profitable recruiting of junior college players. He brought in Chris Pervall, a promising guard from Coffeyville JC in Kansas, to join two holdover starters, guard Jimmy Rodgers and rangy center George Peeples. It was Pervall's 27 points that triggered the victory over UCLA. Iowa had seldom scored over 100 points in a basketball game, but Miller quickly changed that, too—more than once. In the days before the scoreboard could go that high, the Hawks raced away to a school-record 111–68 victory at home against Michigan State and tied the mark a few weeks later by outscoring Purdue, 111–85.

That would be the first of three straight first-division finishes in the Big Ten. To begin the 1965–66 season, Iowa once again matched the 111-point record and what a curtain-raiser it was. The Hawks pressured Pepperdine into so many early turnovers that they quickly amassed an incredible 32–2 lead. The final score was 111–50. By late December they stood 7–0 and had climbed to number nine in the national polls heading into a game against Texas Western (now Texas–El Paso) in the Sun Bowl Classic.

That was the Texas Western team featured in the movie *Glory Road* for its history-making role in winning the 1966

Father-Son Captains

Iowa has had several father-son basketball players but none with the unique distinction of the Chapmans. When Tom Chapman Jr. captained the Hawkeyes in 1967, he duplicated what his father had done twenty-four years earlier. The senior Chapman was Iowa's captain and leading scorer in 1943.

NCAA championship. The Texans started an all-black lineup in the national final, something that had never happened before, and beat Kentucky's all-white team. The movie plot takes a few liberties with what actually happened in the Iowa game, no doubt for dramatic effect. Supposedly the Texans rallied from an 18-point deficit to edge Iowa by a point, but actually they won handily, 86–68.

Miller admitted he'd had misgivings about his team's lofty rating, and an inability to win on the road proved fatal in the Big Ten race. The Hawks won all their home games that year (12–0), only the third time that had been accomplished in school history, but their road woes sent them skidding to an 8–6 record in the conference, which was still good enough for third place.

Pervall and Peeples, his two scoring leaders, completed their eligibility in 1965. Miller needed some more emergency help, so he dipped back into the junior colleges again for someone who not only became a star but left an indelible mark on Hawkeye basketball. He was Sam Williams, a player who had no intention of going on to college after graduating from a Detroit high school. Instead, he hauled beef for two years in a cold-storage plant, which finally convinced him there had to be a better way to make a living.

Through some basketball contacts, Miller had recommended that Williams enroll at Burlington Junior College in

Sam Williams receives the Silver Basketball trophy as the Big Ten's most valuable player in 1968 from Chicago Tribune sports editor Cooper Rollow.

southeast Iowa, where Fred Brown would eventually start his rise to fame. When Sam arrived with the Hawkeyes to start the 1966–67 campaign, Miller could see right away that he had a diamond in the rough. Williams was the standout in a rebuilt lineup, averaging 22.6 points, and the Hawks might have snared a piece of the Big Ten title except for a discouraging loss at home in three overtimes to Wisconsin, 96–95. That snapped a twenty-one-game home winning streak, and Iowa eventually had to settle for third place in the conference once again.

Then came the breakthrough year when Williams guided the Hawks to a Big Ten co-championship with Ohio State, both teams notching 10–4 league records. The arrival of Calabria and Vidnovoc provided a major boost, but Sam was the driveshaft. He averaged 25.3 points and was named the Big Ten's most valuable player—Iowa's last winner of that award.

Unfortunately, the season ended on two downers. Despite Williams's 30 points and 14 rebounds, Iowa was unable to wrap up sole possession of the championship, losing its home finale to Michigan, 74–70. In prior years that still would have been good enough for the Hawks to represent the Big Ten in the NCAA tournament, because Ohio State had been there more recently, but the conference changed the rules before that season, and a playoff was stipulated to break championship ties. Iowa had won their only meeting of the regular season, but when the teams met again on a neutral floor at Purdue, it was Ohio State that claimed the NCAA prize, 81–75.

Based on career averages, Williams is Iowa's all-time top scorer with a 24-point mark in forty-nine games over his two seasons. In 2002 he was one of twenty players chosen on the school's All-Century team. Johnson and Brown also earned that distinction from the players of the Miller era.

After Johnson hooked up with holdover starters Calabria, Vidnovic, and Chris Phillips the next season, things didn't materialize as expected. Miller's Hawks fell back to eighth place. But with the arrival of Brown for the 1969–70 season, the Hawkeyes found their missing link.

Lute, Lute, Lute

Lute Olson was disillusioned and more than a little angry. Here he was, almost forty years old, and he feared his coaching career in Division I college basketball might be over almost before it started.

Olson had toiled in the high school and junior college ranks for a number of years before he got what he thought was his big break in the summer of 1973. Jerry Tarkanian, head coach at Long Beach State, left to take the coaching job at Nevada–Las Vegas, leaving

behind a myriad of problems for his successor—and that was Olson. Unaware of how serious the recruiting violations had been at Long Beach State, Lute left his coaching position at Los Angeles City College to replace the man they called "Tark the Shark."

He enjoyed a good first season, too, posting a 24–2 record. But as it turned out, the Long Beach State administrators had not leveled with their new coach. They failed to tell him the NCAA was about to throw the book at them for all of Tarkanian's misdeeds. "They lied to me," says Olson. "They led me to believe that the problems were not serious, when in fact the NCAA was about to put the school on three years probation. I didn't feel I could stay there after they'd done that to me. I figured I would try to get my old City College job back or maybe go back to the high schools."

Olson is a native Midwesterner, growing up in the small town of Mayville, North Dakota. He played college basketball at Augsburg in Minneapolis and coached for six years at two Minnesota high schools before moving to California. He continued teaching and coaching in the Los Angeles area before moving up to City College and then to nearby Long Beach State. And that's where he stood, at a coaching crossroads in the spring of 1974, when a most unusual thing happened.

Coach Lute Olson discusses strategy with budding Iowa star Greg Stokes.

Out of Nowhere—a Victory!

There was no reason to think Iowa had much chance to beat Purdue when the teams met in Iowa City on February 11, 1974. The hapless Hawkeyes had lost eight straight games and were at the bottom of the Big Ten with a 1–6 record. Purdue was tied for first at 7–1.

Dick Schultz was in his fourth and last season as Iowa's head coach, so the Hawks seemed to be doing nothing more than just playing out the string. But what transpired was the wildest, highest-scoring game in the history of Iowa Fieldhouse. Iowa won in three overtimes, 112–111.

The game was tied at the end of regulation play, 81–81, and then at 92–92 after one extra period, and again at 101–101 after two. Nate Washington, a 6'6" football player who had decided to come out for basketball that winter, finally ended the fifty-five-minute marathon by hitting the winning basket with 9 seconds left in the third overtime.

He received a telephone call from a University of Iowa fan, Al Schallau, a former Iowa City resident who was living in the Los Angeles area. Schallau had just heard that Dick Schultz had been fired as Iowa's basketball coach, and he thought Olson would be an ideal candidate for the Hawkeyes. Schallau said he had seen Lute's teams play at City College and at Long Beach State, he'd been impressed with them, and wondered if Lute would be interested in the Iowa job. "Are you kidding?" Schallau said he was told. "It's always been my dream to coach in the Big Ten."

Coaching positions in big-time college basketball just aren't filled that easily, of course, but Schallau followed through by calling Bump Elliott, the Iowa athletic director, and recommending this almost unknown coach on the West Coast. Schallau said not only were Olson's teams well coached, but Olson also was impressive in TV interviews.

Elliott thanked Schallau for taking the time to call, saying that he appreciated the recommendation and would certainly look into it. More times than not in such situations, there is no more story. The athletic director already has another candidate or two in mind, and some fan's choice from a far-off place seldom stands much chance. But Elliott called several men he respected in college basketball, including longtime coach Pete Newell, and heard nothing but glowing words of praise for Olson. "I called Lute to see if he'd be interested in coming in for an interview," Bump recalled. "He was in Denver on a recruiting trip and said he would just come on from there. I remember it was spring break and there was nobody around. Usually word spreads quickly in coaching searches, but we'd go out to dinner and nobody knew who he was."

It wouldn't take long for that to change. After Olson was given the job and his teams began to appear regularly on TV, he became one of the most popular and recognizable figures in Iowa. Chants of "Lute, Lute, Lute" soon rocked the Fieldhouse on game nights.

"It's funny how things work out," Olson says of Schallau's phone call. "It sure worked out well for me."

The two men became friends after that, and Schallau says proudly, "Now whenever I'm with Lute, he introduces me as the guy who got him the Iowa job. I've often wondered over the years what would have happened if Bump had not taken my call that day, or if I was told to call back later. I wouldn't have called back, Lute wouldn't have coached at Iowa, and there might not even be a Carver-Hawkeye Arena."

Olson arrived in the Big Ten at a time when Indiana and its coach, Bobby Knight, were riding high, posting successive 18–0 records to win conference titles in 1975 and 1976 and winning the 1976 national championship. Bruce "Sky" King was the Iowa standout in that period, totaling over 1,300 points for Olson's first three teams. The Hawks rose from 10–16 in 1975 to 19–10 the next year and a 9–9 conference record good enough for fifth place.

Ronnie Lester seems to float on air as he rifles a pass to a teammate. Coach Olson looks on in the background.

And then came a major recruiting breakthrough—one of the most important in Olson's long career. Lute snared a young point guard out of Chicago, Ronnie Lester, to run his offense for the next four years. Lester became an immediate starter as a freshman, led the Hawks to a Big Ten co-championship in his junior year, and then overcame a serious knee injury to carry them all the way to the Final Four in 1980. Olson still rates Lester as the finest point guard he's coached—and he's had some very good ones in his years at Arizona. "For speed and quickness and overall ability, I'd have to say Ronnie was the best," says Lute. "He was just so explosive."

The Hawks had slipped to eighth place in Lester's sophomore year, so not much was expected from them in 1979. They were picked to finish eighth again. Michigan State and Magic Johnson were supposed to be the kingpins, along with Michigan and Minnesota. But Iowa won nine of its first eleven games and stayed in the Big Ten title picture all the way. Lester averaged 18.7 points in earning All-America honors and was at his brilliant best in a late-season showdown at Ohio State. In addition to the game's importance in the team standings, it was a personal duel between the two best point guards in the league, Lester and Ohio State's Kelvin Ransey.

The Buckeyes had won the earlier meeting in Iowa City, but Lester turned in a flawless performance this time as Iowa took the rematch, 83–68. His line in the box score went like this: 13 for 19 from the field, 5 for 5 from the line, 31 points, 9 assists, 4 rebounds, and 3 steals in thirty-nine minutes. Ransey led Ohio State with 22 points.

That game was the difference in letting Iowa share the conference title with Michigan State and Purdue. All had 13–5 records. Ohio State wound up fourth at 12–6. The surprising Hawks didn't last long in the NCAA tournament, however, going to the sidelines in the first round with a 74–72 loss at the hands of Toledo.

An Ugly Game

Midway through the 1980 season, Michigan State coach Jud Heathcote apparently felt the best chance his team had to beat Iowa was to hold the ball and keep the score down. So he ordered the Spartans to stall from the outset, drawing a chorus of boos from a sellout crowd in Iowa Fieldhouse. The halftime score was Iowa 8, Michigan State 6.

If ever there was an argument in favor of a shot clock in college basketball, that was it. The pace picked up slightly in the second half and regulation play ended in a 31–31 tie, with Iowa prevailing in the extra period, 44–39. The Hawks used only five players, Michigan State six.

Lester's senior season in 1980 began with high hopes. Olson had a solid cast to go with him. Steve Waite and Steve Krafcisin were a strong pair of 6'10" players in the front line, Vince Brookins was a solid outside shooter, and Kevin Boyle had started every game as a freshman the year before. Kenny Arnold was counted on to be a valuable contributor, along with incoming freshmen Bobby Hansen and Mark Gannon.

The Hawks won their first eight preconference games, but at that point the season began to unravel with a steady string of damaging injuries, beginning in the eighth game at Dayton when Lester suffered a severe knee injury. He was gone indefinitely. Arnold, already playing with a broken thumb, moved from shooting guard to take over at the point, and Iowa managed to make it ten in row by winning a one-pointer at Illinois.

Then came the decline, starting with close losses to Michigan and Ohio State. Along about that time Gannon was lost for the season with a ligament tear in his knee. Hansen suffered a broken hand, but, like Arnold, he continued playing. So did Krafcisin although he was bothered by an assortment of injuries. "I think John Streif, our trainer, was the MVP that year," said Hansen. "He was always taping us together so we could keep playing."

Olson can't remember a season quite like it. "You always have injuries. One year at Iowa we lost William Mayfield and Clay Hargrave with broken hands in the same game. But 1980 — that was really a tough year."

Hawkeyes Kenny Arnold (30) and Steve Krafcisin defend against Indiana star Isiah Thomas.

Lester tried a comeback in midseason but lasted only two games before he hurt the knee again, requiring minor surgery. Without him the Hawks struggled to an 8–8 conference record heading into the final two games, both at home against Michigan and Illinois. Their chances of making the NCAA tournament were no better than 50–50 even if they won those two games. They took care of Michigan, 83–67, by shooting a torrid 65 percent to set a Fieldhouse record.

The Illinois finale was senior day, and Lester was the only senior. Iowa made it an extra special occasion by retiring his jersey number twelve, and Ronnie responded by also playing in the game, with Olson telling him not to put any pressure on the tender knee, just to pass and shoot. His return raised the spirits of his teammates, and they knocked off the Illini, 75–71.

With Lester back in the fold, and because Iowa had won six of its last nine games, the NCAA selection committee slipped the unranked Hawks into the postseason field as one of the last at-large choices. But the committee did them no favors by sending them to Greensboro, North Carolina, where the first-round opponent was Virginia Commonwealth. Right away they proved they'd be hard for anyone to handle by winning that game, 86–72, with Arnold scoring 23 points and Lester, Waite, and Boyle each hitting 17. Next up was North Carolina State, and the rejuvenated Hawks again used a balanced attack to win going away, 77–64. Arnold had 18 points, Lester and Vince Brookins, 17 each.

Then it was on to the Spectrum in Philadelphia for the Sweet Sixteen. How long would this run continue? Not much longer, probably, because number one seed Syracuse was waiting there. But Iowa did it again, shooting better than 50 percent for the fifth straight game to claim an 88–77 victory. The Cinderella Hawkeyes were one game away from the Final Four. Georgetown, the number two seed, would be next.

The hot-shooting battle between those two teams was something to see. There were long stretches when neither side missed. Iowa hit 70.8 percent of its shots in the second half (17 of 24 attempts) and 60.8 percent for the game. But would you believe it, Georgetown was even better! The Hoyas shot 62 percent. Iowa rallied from a 14-point deficit in the last half, and everything came down to the closing seconds, with the score tied at 78–78 and the Hawks in possession of the ball. Big Steve Waite will be forever remembered for what happened next. "Time was running out when Kevin Boyle drove the lane but was shut off," Waite explained. "That left me open on the side, about 12 to 15 feet away, and he passed off to me. I dribbled across the lane, used my shoulder to protect my left side, and was fouled as I scored on a close shot."

Five seconds remained and the resulting free throw would all but clinch the upset victory, since there was no three-point shot in college basketball at that time. Georgetown took a time-out in an attempt to freeze Waite, and Bobby Hansen said he didn't help matters in the sideline huddle by shouting at his teammate, "Make the free throw, make the free throw."

Waite didn't need to be reminded of its importance but said he felt calm, cool, and collected. "I wasn't the greatest free thrower in the world, but I hadn't missed one in that game and felt confident. I told Bobby, 'Don't worry about it, I'm okay.'" He calmly dropped in the vital point (Waite was 4 for 4 from the field, 7 for 7 from the line that afternoon), and Iowa walked off an 81–80 winner after Georgetown added a last-second basket.

With Lester's knee holding up, Olson's Hawks had to be considered as a title threat when the Final Four got under way at Market Square Arena in Indianapolis. For one of the few times ever, all the regional number one seeds were eliminated along the way, putting Iowa in the semifinals against Louisville, and another Big Ten team, Purdue, facing UCLA.

By this time Lester seemed to be his old self, but then, after twelve minutes during which he scored 10 points and made all four of his shots from the floor, he came down hard on the bad leg and his knee crumpled under him. When he was helped from the floor, it marked a sad ending to his exceptional Hawkeye career and doomed Iowa's chances of winning the big prize. Louisville's Darrell Griffith proved to be a one-man wrecking crew with a 34-point barrage, leading the Cardinals to an 80–72 victory. Louisville topped UCLA in the championship game, 59–54, and Joe Barry Carroll's 35 points powered Purdue over Iowa for third place, 75–58.

Olson had a solid foundation returning, losing only Lester from that Final Four team, and Big Ten championships were tantalizingly close in the next three years—three consecutive runner-up teams, each of which ran into hard-luck finishes in late-season games. The 1981 outfit beat eventual champion Indiana twice during the season but they lost a chance to tie or win the title outright, losing by a single point in overtime at Michigan State, then suffering a season-ending setback at Ohio State.

Three straight losses to close out the 1982 season furnished much the same story: the first in three overtimes at home to Minnesota, the next in overtime at Illinois after the Hawks squandered a big lead, and the third a galling 66–65 loss at Purdue in the famed "Jim Bain Incident." Olson went ballistic at the end of that one after Bain whistled a phantom foul on Kevin Boyle following a rebound scramble under Iowa's basket. Boyle was not near the disputed play, as TV reruns clearly showed, and with time expired and the score deadlocked at 65, Purdue won the game on a free throw resulting from the Bain call.

"You can chalk this one up to Bain and his crew," an irate Olson said afterward, "Kenny Arnold drove for the basket and got absolutely hammered, yet there was no guts on anyone's part to make the call. It's an absolute disgrace for people to steal basketball games from people this way. When officials don't see the call, they should not make it."

Lute made some other choice comments, such as the officials "deserve to be in jail," and Bain "obviously needs a cane." Later, he learned that Bain not only worked the Iowa-Purdue game in the afternoon, he flew his plane back from West Lafayette to Kansas City to officiate the Big Eight Conference tournament championship game that night. Bain also had worked a game in Kansas City the night before.

"On top of making a ridiculous call in our game," Olson says now, "it was very unprofessional of him to accept two officiating assignments on the same day—and they were nowhere near each other. That was very unprofessional, but he paid for it in the long run."

Bain later admitted to friends that he had been promised the job as Big Ten supervisor of basketball officials, but in the aftermath of the Iowa-Purdue game, that was denied him. The Big Ten office was flooded with more than 7,500 letters from angry Iowa

A Stricken Teammate

Kenny Arnold, one of the standouts on Iowa's 1980 Final Four team, underwent surgery for a malignant brain tumor a few years after his playing career ended, and he's been in a fight to regain his health ever since. Former teammates have come to his aid, raising more than $50,000 to help defray medical expenses and to assist in his rehabilitation. Lute Olson, who was Arnold's coach at Iowa, reportedly has contributed a significant sum to the fund. The former Hawkeyes also played a benefit game in the spring of 2006 that raised $17,000. After learning several years ago that Arnold was in dire financial straits, some of his ex-teammates hired an attorney who won disability benefits that had previously been denied him.

fans protesting Bain's phantom call, and he was later forced to cancel a speaking engagement in the Quad Cities after receiving a death threat. Although he continued to officiate conference games, he was not assigned to any involving Iowa for several years.

Tough luck continued to dog the Hawks in the NCAA tournament after the 1982 season, when they were taken into overtime and bounced out by Idaho in the second round, 69–67.

The next year marked the start of a new era in Iowa basketball. Greg Stokes and Michael Payne, known as the Twin Towers, moved into the starting lineup, and the Hawks not only said good-bye to the Iowa Fieldhouse with the opening of Carver-Hawkeye Arena, but also bid a fond farewell to their coach. Olson moved on to Arizona after Iowa's third straight runner-up finish in the Big Ten. As it developed, his coaching career was just getting up a full head of steam. It's amazing how one phone call has the power to change a person's life.

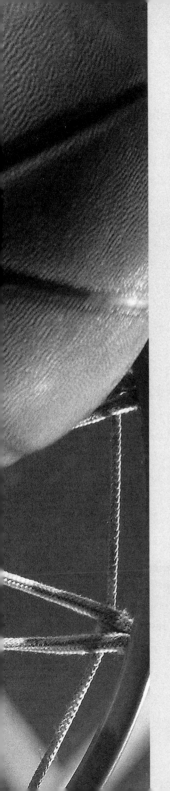

Basketball in Prime Time

It didn't take Lute Olson long after his arrival as Iowa's head basketball coach to begin campaigning for a new arena to replace the venerable and outdated Fieldhouse. He found it difficult to interest promising young athletes to play for the Hawkeyes when other schools could entice them with much more modern structures.

The Fieldhouse did have its a good points, of course, not the least of which was a powerful home-court advantage when sell-out crowds would shake the rafters with ear-splitting roars and their foot-stomping racket. They could pump extra adrenaline into the home forces and deflate even the most worthy of opponents. "I always said it would be nice if we could play our games in the Fieldhouse and recruit to the new arena," says Olson.

There were simply too many negatives to keep playing indefinitely in the Fieldhouse. The bleacher-type seats were tough on the rear end and hard on the back, and many had obstructed views because of pillars that held up the balcony. The dusty dirt floor in the adjacent Armory didn't help matters, either, and the locker facilities under the North Gym were antiquated without much hope of improvement.

Two things happened that hastened the coming of a new arena. First, Olson's teams began winning. Their games became a hot ticket. Fans were knocking down the doors to see new stars like Ronnie Lester and to watch Iowa contend for Big Ten championships. Second, and just as important, a man named Bill Bolster decided the time was right to form a statewide network and show all the Iowa games on television.

Bolster was the general manager of KWWL-TV, an NBC affiliate in Waterloo. He got commitments from other NBC stations in Des Moines, Davenport, and Mason City, plus the CBS affiliate in Sioux City, to join his flagship station for what was basically a revolutionary concept. Remember, there was no cable in those days, no ESPN, no FOX Sports—not much of anything other than the three major networks and public TV.

You might think, hey, that's a great idea. And it would turn out to be that way. Initially, however, there was some resistance on Iowa's part. This was unknown territory and giving the games away for free might have a negative impact on ticket sales. Nobody knew for sure. "You always wonder if the weather might hurt the crowd, when people could just stay home and watch on TV," said Bump Elliott, Iowa's athletic director at the time. "But there was also the reverse. The coaches wanted to get the exposure to help recruiting. In the end it was no problem at all. Our games became more popular than ever."

Once he convinced Iowa officials to go along with his plan, Bolster said he knew he had a winner. "Where I got my first inkling of just how big this could be was when we televised an Iowa wrestling meet in Waterloo," he explained. "Gary Kurdelmeier was the Iowa coach and Dan Gable had just joined his staff. We got a huge viewing audience.

"I think it was the following summer, I was standing at the bar after an I-Club golf outing in Waterloo, and Lute was complaining about how tough he was finding it recruiting players. 'I can't even recruit players in the state of Iowa,' he said. And that's when I hatched my idea for a statewide network."

Olson, of course, was all for it. The more exposure the better. "Ralph Miller and some of the others had been opposed to giving the games away on TV," said Lute. "I felt just the opposite. It would add fan appeal. I was sure it would build crowds instead of keeping fans away."

Not only did it build fan appeal, Bolster said, it created a phenomenon. TV ratings for the Iowa games headed into the strato-

Iowa's new arena and the advent of televised home games vastly increased the Hawkeye basketball fan base.

sphere. More than half the sets in the state were tuned into the Hawkeyes on game nights, maybe as many as 75 percent, and Lute Olson became a huge celebrity almost overnight.

"If I had to choose a coach for what we were doing, I couldn't have handpicked a guy better than Lute," Bolster said. "Here was this tall, good-looking guy standing on the sidelines—just a stunning man. He looked like what everybody would want for a son, everybody's brother, and of course he was a heartthrob for the women. And his wife, Bobbi, looked even better."

With the talented Lester leading the way, Iowa climbed out of the second division in the Big Ten in one year and to a co-championship in 1979. What followed was the injury-plagued year in 1980, when the Hawks furnished reality TV at its best on their way to the Final Four.

"As hard as it may seem to young people today, back in those days many people around the state had never seen an Iowa basketball game," said George Wine, Iowa's sports information director emeritus. "When Lute's teams started winning, and there was a lot of excitement, people would say, 'Hey, that looks like fun. I'd like to see a game there.' That's when I knew we had a good thing going—when people would call wanting to get tickets. I started getting a lot of those calls.

"Our games even preempted the *Cosby Show*, which was the number one show on TV back then. That's how popular the games were. In 1979 through the early '80s, I think we had something like 75 to 80 percent of the audience in Iowa. They were numbers the TV brass in New York just couldn't believe."

Wine also gave an interesting sidelight about the first TV play-by-play announcer. Bob Hogue was the KWWL-TV sports anchor, and Bolster wanted him to do the broadcasts. "Bob had never done play-by-play before," said Wine. "So the first time he did play-by-play of a basketball game was the first statewide network game he broadcast."

Bolster said his first contract with Iowa was a three-year deal for $250,000, with the stipulation that if NBC picked up any of the games for the network, he would receive a rebate from Iowa for $40,000 each time that happened.

"After a while the Iowa games had become so popular and so many of them were going to the network that the rebates were going to make up for the whole contract," Bolster recalled. "But we couldn't do it. My boss, Harry Slife, was on the Board of Regents. I went to Harry and told him we were going to wind up getting these games for free, but he said, 'No, we can't do that.' He was afraid of a conflict of interests and we never took any rebate money."

Few Big Ten schools had TV packages in those days, but they soon saw the benefits that Iowa was reaping, both in exposure and revenue. Others began to put together their own deals, and before the situation got totally out of hand, the conference decided it would be best and more equal to have one main package shared by all.

"I remember, at a conference meeting we had to determine what we should do," said Elliott. "Should we go with the Big Ten package or stick with our own, which was a better deal financially? We decided it would be better to go along with the Big Ten. We could still televise our own games if we weren't picked for a Big Ten network game, much as the situation is now in football and basketball."

After Iowa shared the conference title in 1979, along with all the TV success, Olson had good reason to push ahead and convince Hawkeye officials that it was past time for the university to build a new arena. While plans were being formulated in 1980, Olson, Elliott, and others began touring arenas around the country to get some ideas on what kind of a facility they wanted to fill vacant land west of University Hospitals. They made fund-raising trips around Iowa to raise money for a projected 15,500-seat building, which would cost in the neighborhood of $17 million.

Shortly after construction began on the three-year project, Roy Carver, who was one of the university's biggest benefactors and a Hawkeye sports enthusiast, died unexpectedly at the age of seventy-one. Carver was a multimillionaire industrialist who had founded the Bandag Company in nearby Muscatine. He left part of his fortune to the university and some of this money, about $5 million, was earmarked for the arena—hence the name Carver-Hawkeye Arena.

It was hoped that the new facility, which included athletic offices for all sports (football was later moved to its own complex), would be ready for the start of the 1982–83 basketball season. Construction delays pushed back the opening until January 1983, after Iowa had opened with four nonconference victories in the Fieldhouse. The Hawks beat USC, 66–55, in the last official game played in the old building.

Meanwhile, Coach Dan Gable's wrestlers, in the midst of winning nine straight NCAA championships, had the honor of hosting the first competition in Carver-Hawkeye Arena—which many found appropriate, since Roy Carver was such a devoted wrestling fan. Gable's team, which hardly ever lost a meet in that

Women Set Carver Record

Iowa's women set the basketball attendance record for Carver-Hawkeye Arena when they drew an overflow crowd of 22,157 for a game against Ohio State on February 3, 1985, setting a national single-game record for women.

It was a special pack-the-house promotion, and Hawkeye fans responded in such numbers that the gates finally were thrown open to admit all comers. All the aisles were jammed with spectators and the upper concourse was filled with standees. Fire officials looked the other way but warned Iowa not to do something like that again.

The Carver-Hawkeye men's single-game record of 15,570 was set when Iowa beat Indiana, 101–88, in 1987. A national record for a dual wrestling meet was established in 1983, the first year Carver-Hawkeye was opened, when 15,283 spectators saw Iowa top Iowa State, 26–11.

era, ushered in the new facility by routing Oklahoma, 35–7, on January 3, 1983.

Two nights later, Olson's basketballers weren't as fortunate. I remember covering the game and this is how I started my story in the *Des Moines Register:*

> Iowa City, Ia.—When they said Carver-Hawkeye Arena wasn't finished, they weren't kidding. Somebody forgot to take the lid off the basket. So what was supposed to be a happy occasion Wednesday night, the first basketball game in a $17.2 million building, turned into a nightmare for eighth-ranked Iowa as the cold-shooting Hawkeyes were upset by Michigan State, 61–59.

The game had a stunning finish. The crowd of 15,283—it was announced as a sellout although there were some empty seats, with the students away on vacation—let out a mighty roar when Bobby Hansen swished a three-point shot that apparently let Iowa win with only 2 seconds left. But the officials ruled Steve Carfino had stepped out of bounds on the sideline before passing the ball to Hansen. No basket. No victory.

Iowa lost two other close games at home that season, one in two overtimes to Ohio State and the other a two-pointer to Minnesota. The Hawks finished tied for second place in the conference that year but might have won or shared the title with Indiana had they made a better home showing—which immediately led to speculation that they'd lost a big advantage by moving out of the Fieldhouse.

Iowa's "Twin Towers," Greg Stokes (41) and Michael Payne (42) go to work under the basket.

Statistics over a long period of time have proved that thinking to be a fallacy, however. Iowa is winning at a faster clip in twenty-four years at Carver-Hawkeye Arena (.793) than the old-timers did in fifty-seven years at the Fieldhouse (.732). Veteran observers believe when the modern-day fans are revved up in the newer building; with a capacity of about 2,000 more, the decibel level is even higher than it was in the so-called good old days.

The 1983 season was to be Olson's last before he departed for his long and successful run at Arizona. For the third straight year, Iowa finished in the Big Ten's runner-up spot. Led by a pair of sophomores who became known as the Twin Towers, Greg Stokes and Michael Payne, the team posted an overall record of 22–9. Stokes went on to set a Hawkeye career scoring mark with 1,768 points in four years and was later picked on Iowa's All-Century team. Iowa advanced to the Sweet Sixteen of the NCAA tournament in 1983 before losing a one-point game to Villanova.

Olson had made no secret of the fact that he planned to head back for warmer climes some day; he was just waiting for the right situation to come along. Earlier in his Iowa stay he turned down an offer from Southern California—for one thing, USC didn't have its own basketball facility at that time—but he was much more receptive to Arizona's offer.

While Olson was still the Iowa coach, the Big Ten and several other conferences began experimenting with two major rule changes: the three-point shot, to reward outside shooters as well as add some excitement for teams playing catch-up in the late stages, and a shot clock to prevent long and boring stalls. Both those features had been a part of the professional game for many years. In 1983 the Big Ten tried the three-point shot for one year, and Iowa's Steve Carfino was the conference leader with twenty-seven long-range baskets in eighteen games. The league did not do it again until the NCAA approved the rule in 1987. And the leader that year, incidentally, was an Indiana All-American, Steve Alford, who later became the Iowa coach. He doubled Carfino's output with fifty-four three-pointers.

Instituting a shot clock in college basketball did not come without a fight, and many of the game's purists are still opposed to it. Forcing teams to shoot in a certain amount of time limits the opportunity to set up offensive strategy, goes the argument, and the sport was all right the way it was. Why copy what the pros were doing? But the rule makers felt they had to do something to counteract deliberate stalling that had become so objectionable. One Atlantic Coast Conference game was an incredible 7–0 at the half, and Iowa had a slow-motion halftime lead of 8–6 in a 1980 game. When the NCAA finally went to a shot clock in 1986, rather than make a drastic change to the NBA 24-second clock, it adopted a much more liberal 45-second clock. This was lowered to 35 seconds in 1993. The international rule is 30 seconds, which is the time used in NCAA women's games.

When Olson left in March 1983, Iowa looked once again to the West Coast and chose George Raveling, a popular and gregarious coach who had spent the previous eleven years at Washington State. Raveling seemed to be a good choice to take advantage of the groundwork Olson had done, and with his proven recruiting ability, he would probably add to it. He was an African American who related well to black athletes.

As it developed, he laid some important groundwork of his own but did not stick around to see just how good his new play-

Almost Perfect

Iowa began hosting a December basketball tournament in 1982, which was supposed to celebrate the opening of Carver-Hawkeye Arena, but which had to be delayed for a month. The Hawks won the first two games of the Hawkeye Invitational in the old Fieldhouse, and since moving into the arena, they've proved almost unbeatable. Their only loss in the tournament's first forty-eight games was to Arkansas State in 1986.

ers were. In 1985 he brought in an all-star cast of freshmen— probably the best recruiting class in Iowa history. It included Roy Marble, a three-time all-state player in Michigan and a McDonald's All-American; Ed Horton, Illinois's Mr. Basketball and another McDonald's All-American; and B. J. Armstrong, another highly touted all-stater from Michigan. That trio became household names in Iowa and both Marble and Armstrong were picked on Iowa's All-Century team. Before their careers really flowered, however, Raveling decided that small-town life in Iowa City didn't suit him, and after only three seasons, he moved to Los Angeles and took the USC job.

Raveling's first Hawkeye season in 1984 did not come up to expectations. The team lost eleven of its first thirteen conference games and slipped to seventh place in the Big Ten, winding up below .500 at 13–15 overall. But the next season saw a sharp turnaround, with Stokes and Payne in their senior years and with the addition of muscular Gerry Wright and freshman sharpshooter Jeff Moe. Stokes furnished a good bit of the offense with a 19.9 average, and the Hawks notched a 21–11 record, including 10–8 for fifth in the conference.

Then came that all-star recruiting class. The 6'6" Marble, a great leaper around the basket, became an immediate starter, and although he averaged a modest 12.5 points per game, it was good enough to lead the team's balanced scoring. Wright, Andre Banks, and sophomore Al Lorenzen all averaged between 10.0 and 10.7, and the Hawks wound up at 20–12.

So Raveling was leaving the cupboard well stocked when he made his surprising departure for Southern California.

The Tom Davis Years

Tom Davis knew he had inherited a bunch of promising young players from George Raveling when he became the Iowa coach in 1986, but if he needed any convincing, he got it from North Carolina State coach Jim Valvano. The two old friends had met in an airport somewhere in their recruiting travels shortly after Tom had accepted the Hawkeye post.

"Jim had been the Bucknell coach when I was at Lafayette so we'd known each other a long time," Davis related. "His North Carolina State team had played Iowa in the NCAA tournament that year, and he told me, 'Tom, the group of athletes you're getting is ideal for your system,' and he sure was right. They were not only talented physically, they were real competitors, they got along well with each other, and they made for a very good team atmosphere."

It would be a long time before Davis lost a game as the Iowa coach. The youthful Hawkeyes reeled off eighteen straight victories to start the 1986–87 season, setting a school record that still stands, beating the mark of seventeen by the famed Fabulous Five in 1956.

Sophomores Roy Marble, Ed Horton, and B. J. Armstrong were the big guns, along with a pair of seniors, 7'0" Brad Lohaus and long-range shooter Kevin Gamble. Davis coached an up-tempo style and Jeff Moe, Gerry Wright, and Al Lorenzen were others who got plenty of playing time.

The agile Marble and the brawny Horton were dominating players around the basket. Marble had been the player of the year as a high school senior in Michigan, and Horton came in after being voted Mr. Basketball in Illinois. Although Armstrong also was headed for stardom with the Hawks and later with the Chicago Bulls, he was a large question mark as the potential point guard. Raveling did not use him much as a freshman and, in fact, told friends privately that he might have made a mistake in recruiting B. J. "The way I like to play, point guard is critical to the fast break," said Davis, "making decisions when to run and when to slow it down. We opened that year against the Russian National team on ESPN—those exhibition games were a big deal back then—and B. J. answered any questions I had and his teammates had whether he could play point guard at that level."

Tom Davis won his first eighteen games as head basketball coach at Iowa.

Number One in the Draft

Iowa has had seven players picked in the first round of
the NBA draft over the years, including two in 1989:
B. J. Armstrong by Chicago and Roy Marble by Atlanta.
Other Hawkeyes who were first-round draft picks: John
Johnson, 1970, Cleveland; Fred Brown, 1971, Seattle;
Kevin Kunnert, 1973, Chicago; Ronnie Lester, 1980,
Portland; Ricky Davis, 1998, Charlotte.

And then there's Matt Bullard. He was not drafted in
1990, went into the NBA as a free agent, and spent
eleven years with various teams, mostly with Houston.

The season began with a trip to the Great Alaska Shootout
and an opening victory over Alaska-Anchorage. Then as luck
would have it, the second-round opponent was North Carolina
State, where Jim Valvano would see firsthand just how prophetic
his words had been. Iowa upset his seventeenth-ranked Wolfpack
in overtime, 90–89. Michael Reeves was supposed to be the
Hawkeye point guard, but he hurt a knee, letting Armstrong
move into the starting lineup. And what a debut! In addition to
directing traffic, B. J. scored 26 points, making 9 of 16 shots,
including 5 out of 6 on three-pointers, and going 3 of 4 on free
throws. "I don't know how you can expect a young sophomore
point guard to play any better," gushed Davis.

Iowa was 14 points down with less than five minutes to play before outscoring the Wolfpack down the stretch, 20–6, forcing the overtime on Armstrong's last-second free throws. Big Lohaus's clutch free throw won it with 3 seconds left in the extra period. Iowa went on to win the tournament by routing Northeastern in the championship game, 103–80, shooting a school-record 69.8 percent. Davis obviously had a powerhouse in the making. Marble led the way with 29 points (9 of 11 on field goals), and Moe came off the bench to hit 26 (5 of 6 three-pointers).

From there the winning streak mounted into January until it reached eighteen with consecutive victories over three nationally ranked opponents—number eight Illinois, number five Purdue, and number three Indiana. By that time Iowa had climbed to number one in the country. But then came a rude awakening, an 80–76 loss at home to lightly regarded Ohio State. "Maybe the players feel relieved that the streak is over, but I don't," Davis said afterward. "I'm sorry it ended. I was worried that the players didn't realize that Ohio State ranks right up there with Purdue, Illinois, and Indiana. I told them, but I don't think I was heard."

Several weeks later came another damaging defeat on the home court, an 80–73 setback at the hands of Purdue, and this was critical in the final Big Ten standings. Purdue and Indiana shared the championship with 15–3 conference records, and Iowa had to settle for third at 14–4.

From there the Hawkeyes sent their fans on a roller coaster of emotions in the NCAA tournament after beginning with an easy first-round victory over Santa Clara. They trailed Texas–El Paso by 7 points in the closing minutes, then rallied to pull out an 84–82 victory. Marble, as was becoming routine, led the way with

The stars of a great recruiting class in 1985, from left: B. J. Armstrong, Ed Horton, and Roy Marble.

28 points. That sent them into the Sweet Sixteen, with the next game against Oklahoma in Seattle's Kingdome.

Once again, they fell behind, first by 16 points in the opening half, then by 5 with two minutes to go before an Armstrong three-pointer sent the game into overtime. They were down 91–90 and seemingly doomed to defeat as the clock ticked under 10 seconds left in the extra period. Armstrong had the ball, searching for open man. He finally found Gamble, and it was desperation time. Gamble let fly with a high, arching shot and lo and behold, he scored one of the most memorable baskets in Hawkeye history, a three-point swisher that gave Iowa a thrilling 93–91 victory.

It was almost as if these Hawks expected to win, no matter how big a hole they'd dug themselves. During the Big Ten season, they were apparently dead and buried at Illinois, trailing by 22 points before surging back to win in overtime, 91–88. Wouldn't it be nice to get a comfortable lead for a change? How about 19 points? Well, that's the margin they built in the first half against number one–ranked Nevada–Las Vegas in the battle to see which team would go to the Final Four. Iowa led the Running Rebels at halftime, 58–42.

But the Hawks were about to see what the other side of the coin looked like. UNLV began pecking away at the Iowa lead, forcing turnovers and hitting three-pointers until they had walked off with an 84–81 victory—an absolute stunner for Hawkeye fans. "That was a crushing loss," says Davis. "UNLV changed its tactics at halftime, going away from a soft defense and getting very aggressive. Kevin Gamble got into foul trouble, and we didn't handle the ball very well coming down the stretch. I've often

wondered, if we hadn't got in foul trouble in the guard court, we might have been able to win the national championship."

Instead, it was Indiana that won the NCAA title, with UNLV finishing third. Davis had been named the Big Ten coach of the year and was later named the AP national coach of the year. Iowa's thirty victories in a 30–5 season remain a school record.

With Marble, Horton, and Armstrong returning for the next two years, Iowa's hopes for a Big Ten championship had seldom been brighter. But even though they soared over the 100-point mark fifteen times the next season, the Hawks could post no better than a 12–6 conference record for a third-place tie, followed by 10–8 for fourth when the standout threesome were seniors. Marble totaled 2,116 points in his four years to set Iowa's existing career scoring record, and both he and Armstrong were named to the school's All-Century team.

Davis slowly built up another title contender for the 1993 season, featuring a shot-blocking whiz in 6'11" senior Acie Earl (he led the Big Ten in blocked shots four years in a row); an extraordinary shooter in another senior, Val Barnes; and a rising star in junior Chris Street. They led the Hawks to twelve victories in their first fourteen starts. At that point in mid-January, Iowa lost a nonconference game to Duke, 65–56, but there was one notable achievement—Street's thirty-fourth consecutive free throw in a six-game stretch, setting a school record that still stood as of 2006.

Hawkeye Acie Earl (55) led the Big Ten in blocked shots four years in a row.

The 6'8" junior didn't have a chance to improve on it in the next game, scheduled against Northwestern in Iowa City on January 20, because he was killed in a tragic automobile accident the night before. Street was leaving a team meal when his car was struck on the driver's side by a snowplow as he was pulling out of a motel drive and onto the highway. Davis still has difficulty in talking about Street's death without getting emotional.

"Chris had a big impact on the state, especially the young players," Davis said. "He represented what the players in this state are all about. He had a lot of influence on them—you could see that just watching the games on television. Who knows how good that kid was going to be. Guys with that kind of talent don't come along very often."

Davis and his coaches held an emergency meeting at the arena to inform the players of what happened. The Northwestern game was postponed until later in the season, and the Wildcats were sent home. Iowa officials, coaches, players, and others close to the team traveled by bus to Street's funeral in his hometown of Indianola, south of Des Moines. "That was tough," Davis recalls. "The thing that helped me so much was the power and strength shown by Chris's parents, Mike and Patty Street. You know, when you feel your own grief, you just looked at them and tried to imagine how it must feel for them. They were strong through it all, and I think that helped a lot of the players. I know it did the coaches."

Chris Street (40) goes up to shoot over an opponent's outstretched arm.

The funeral service wound up with the "Iowa Fight Song," and, as you would expect, there wasn't a dry eye in the church.

One of the players most affected by the tragedy was Wade Lookingbill. He not only roomed with Street on the road, he played the same position and thus was elevated into the starting lineup when the Hawks played their next game, a road test at Michigan State. Iowa was ranked eleventh in the country, but this would not be the same team, of course, after the loss of Street and the resulting trauma to the others.

"I know the word miracle is overused," Lookingbill said, "but it certainly was a miracle the way we won that game. We were 16 or 18 points down with three and a half minutes to go, and then Val Barnes hit some key three-pointers and Acie Earl came up big in the overtime. Michigan State was pretty good that year, and Eric Snow was a heck of a player, but he was a horrible free thrower. He missed free throw after free throw that helped us catch up."

The Hawks said they won the game as a tribute to Street, but they made it hard for themselves with their sluggish early play. It took them a long time to zero in on the task at hand. "We wanted to play well, but we didn't do it at the start," said Barnes, who wound up with 29 points.

Then it was back home for one of the most emotional games ever in Carver-Hawkeye Arena. The opponent couldn't have been much tougher—fifth-ranked Michigan and its great Fab Five, featuring Chris Webber, Jalen Rose, and Juwan Howard. As freshmen the year before, they had taken the Wolverines all the way to the championship game in the NCAA tournament before losing to Duke. Pregame hype was understandable, of course, and as if anyone needed reminding, many students in the sellout throng wore T-shirts with Street's number on them. The shirts said 40—THE SPIRIT CONTINUES.

After a moment of silence, bedlam prevailed for the next forty minutes as Iowa rallied from an early 9–0 deficit to win 88–80. "At one point the crowd was so loud," Marc Hansen wrote in the *Des Moines Register*, "Acie Earl had to pull Kevin Smith into the huddle." Once again it was Barnes leading the attack with 27 points, followed by Earl with 19. The Street family members were sitting in the first row on the sidelines, and at the end the players rushed over to present them with the game ball. "Christopher might have given a little inspiration to these players," said his father, Mike. "Obviously, he probably did. But I'll tell you what—the players did it. They deserve all the credit."

Davis says he couldn't be prouder of the way his squad responded to the adversity. "Winning those two games, I think

Double Trouble

In the 1997 season Iowa guard Andre Woolridge accomplished an unusual feat, leading the Big Ten in both scoring and assists. He averaged 20.9 points and was also tops in assists for the second year in a row with 6.1 per game.

said a lot about what Chris meant to the team, that he was not just another guy, he was an inspiration to his teammates. He was like that in life and obviously was like that in death. His life inspired us. I think that's why he captured the feelings of so many Iowans of all ages. He was a typical Iowan, but he also was somebody who represented the best of what Iowans are all about—the work ethic, the openness, the way we treat people. Chris was about all those things, a fun-loving and caring person."

In an unusual show of support, an Iowa State player even changed his uniform number and wore Street's number 40 the rest of the season. Iowa retired that number at the last home game, and a memorial honoring Street has been placed on the wall of a hallway in Carver-Hawkeye Arena leading from the locker rooms to the playing floor.

After the two emotion-charged victories, the Hawks owned a 14–4 record, but they were about to be dealt a dose of reality. Three straight losses followed, including one to powerful Indiana, the eventual Big Ten champion, for their lone setback of the home season. From there they righted the ship and won eight of their last ten games to finish tied for third in the conference standings.

"We were still a pretty good team without Chris," Lookingbill recalled. "But with him we might have gone a ways in the NCAA tournament. We lost in the second round to Wake Forest because Rodney Rogers [33 points] was too much for us to handle. We didn't have anybody to guard him. Chris would have stopped him."

Iowa slipped a bit in the next several years before Jess Settles— a hard-working player out of the Street mold—and transfer guard

Andre Woolridge, who led the Big Ten in scoring and assists in 1997, drives toward the basket.

Long-Range Bomber

Chris Kingsbury set an Iowa record for three-point baskets in one game with nine against Drake in late November 1994, then tied it three weeks later against Long Island University. The Big Ten record is ten. Kingsbury totaled 117 three-pointers in the 1994–95 season and ranks second in the league record book to a player who collected 119 in the same season, Michigan State's Shawn Respert.

Andre Woolridge led the Hawks back into the first division in 1996. Technically, Iowa shared the conference title with Purdue the following year when Minnesota was stripped of its championship due to a myriad of recruiting violations—but that was far after the fact. Iowa and Purdue had tied for second place, and the conference later ruled that all Minnesota games from the seasons of 1994 to 1999 be wiped out of the record books.

Woolridge had a sparkling three-year career after transferring from Nebraska, so much so that he was among the twenty players honored on Iowa's All-Century team. Other standouts in the late 1990s were Ryan Bowen and Ricky Davis, both of whom have enjoyed good pro careers, Kent McCausland and Dean Oliver.

In a controversial decision, Tom Davis was told in 1998 that his contract would not be renewed after the following season, which was a shock to him and a disappointment to many Hawkeye followers. Although he is Iowa's winningest coach, compiling a 269–140 record in thirteen years, his teams did not win any Big Ten championships, and Athletic Director Bob Bowlsby felt it was time for a change. When the move was announced, it made Davis a lame-duck coach with one season left.

"They announced it because they wanted to go ahead with a search," said Davis, who later became the Drake coach. "In looking back, I wonder why I didn't look for another job right then, but I didn't. I wasn't ready to move. I guess my thinking was that I owed it to the team and the staff to do the best job we could."

A fourth consecutive twenty-win season resulted, capped by two NCAA tournament victories and a trip to the Sweet Sixteen, where the Hawks lost to eventual national champion Connecticut. Davis boasts a distinctive record in NCAA play—never losing a first-round game in eleven appearances at Boston College, Stanford, and Iowa. He compiled a postseason record of 18–11 in NCAA tournament games.

Steve Alford Arrives

Steve Alford was hired to take Iowa to the next level in basketball, meaning a Big Ten championship once in a while and success in the NCAA tournament. He seemed perfect for the task—a former Mr. Basketball in Indiana's high school ranks, an All-American who led Indiana to the 1987 NCAA title, and a rising young college coach fresh from guiding Southwest Missouri to the NCAA's 1999 Sweet Sixteen.

Champion on the Line

Iowa coach Steve Alford is still the most accurate free thrower in Big Ten history, both for a single season and in a career. As an Indiana freshman in 1984, he set a one-season record by making 116 of 126 attempts for a .913 percentage. Then he raised the mark to .921 the next year with 137 of 150. Those remain as the two best ever in the Big Ten.

Alford, who led Indiana to the national championship in 1987, finished with a career percentage of .898 at the line, also a conference record. He connected on 535 of 596 free throw tries in his four years.

How could he miss? He certainly had the credentials, posting a 78–29 record in four years at Manchester College in Indiana (including a 31–1 season), followed by a 78–48 mark in four years at Southwest Missouri. He was handsome. He had a pretty wife and growing family. The world was his oyster.

But succeeding an established coach like Tom Davis was no easy matter. While Davis had not managed to win any Big Ten championships, he regularly kept his teams near the top and most of the time in the first division, during his thirteen years. He

Coach Steve Alford came to Iowa on fans' expectations of Big Ten championships and NCAA tournament success.

left never having lost a first-round game in the NCAA tournament, having made two trips with Boston College and nine with Iowa, and his teams made one Elite Eight appearance and another in the Sweet Sixteen. From that standpoint, it was a tough act to follow.

Alford, who had almost never faced any adversity as a player or coach, suddenly found himself in a number of tough situations while trying to get Iowa on a consistent winning track. Injuries and player defections seemed to plague him every year, but those were minor compared with the problems created by one of his prize recruits, Pierre Pierce. Late in Pierce's freshman season, he was charged with sexual assault in an embarrassing case that hung on until he sat out a redshirt season in 2002–03.

Pierce was an uncommon talent, a 6'4" guard with nimble athletic moves and a promising future, and after he had undergone rehabilitation treatment, Alford gave him a second chance. Unfortunately, Pierce was involved in a similar case midway through the 2005 season. That time he wound up with a two-year prison sentence.

All this did not sit well with the fans, of course, especially because Iowa was showing little progress toward becoming a Big Ten title contender. Alford did have his moments, however, winning two conference tournaments when the odds were stacked against the Hawks, compiling an unmatched 13–5 record in those postseason meets. Still, he owns only one NCAA tournament victory in seven years, and he's won very little fan support. The critical comments on Hawkeye Internet chat rooms have been brutal at times. One disgruntled fan even started his own Web site, calling it "FireSteveAlford.com." Such things would have to bother most people, but Alford insists it doesn't concern him in the least.

"I don't pay any attention to those things," he says. "What the fans say has zero impact on me. I prefer to emphasize the positives. We're the only coaching staff to have six straight winning seasons in the history of the school. We've won two Big Ten postseason tournaments in six years, and our overall record in the tournament is the best in the conference. And we're doing things the right way. That's the important thing.

"I think we've had a pretty good seven years considering everything we've been dealt. Most of the problems have been totally out of my control."

After a mediocre first season, things appeared to be looking up for Alford in the fall of 2000 with the arrival of Reggie Evans, a rugged 6'8" junior college All-American from Coffeyville, Kansas, and the transfer of a former Indiana star, Luke Recker,

Second Best

Iowa's 25–9 record in 2006 ranks second in Hawkeye history for number of victories in one season. The high mark of thirty victories was set in 1987 by the Marble-Horton-Armstrong team that went 30–5.

who had left the Hoosiers for Arizona but then wound up at Iowa because of tragic circumstances.

Recker, a former Indiana Mr. Basketball, felt he wasn't making much headway in his career under Coach Bobby Knight and decided to transfer to Arizona after his sophomore year. His girlfriend planned to transfer with him, and while they were in Colorado in the summer of 1999, on their way to Arizona, they were involved in a horrible traffic accident. One person was killed, Recker suffered head injuries that required 200 stitches, and his girlfriend was paralyzed and confined to a wheelchair. Recker spent one traumatic semester at Arizona but was lonely and wanted to return to the Midwest. He transferred to Iowa because his father lived and worked near Iowa City. The move would bring him closer to his family.

Recker knew he would have only one and a half years of eligibility remaining, although an appeal was lodged with the NCAA and he was eventually given two years. Senior point guard Dean Oliver, along with Recker and Evans, gave Alford a formidable lineup in 2001. The Hawks got off to a 14–2 start, with Recker averaging 18 points a game and Evans cleaning up on the backboards. Midway through the Big Ten race, Iowa stood 6–2 and poised to make a strong title run when fate intervened— Recker was lost for the remainder of the year with a broken knee cap. Without him the Hawks lost seven of their last eight games in the regular season.

That's why what happened next was so amazing. Iowa went into the Big Ten tournament as a decided underdog, having to win a Thursday game to make the eight-team quarterfinals, yet the Hawks swept past Northwestern, Ohio State, Penn State, and then Indiana to capture the title. No team before or since has won four games in four days to take the championship. Evans was the lopsided winner of the tournament's most outstanding player award, scoring a career-high 30 points and grabbing a meet record 18 rebounds in the semifinal rout of Penn State. Brody Boyd, a pint-sized freshman sharpshooter and Recker's replacement, led the way against homestate Indiana with a 22-point barrage. Boyd had been one of the highest scorers in Indiana high school history for the small town of Dugger, so it wasn't like the Hoosiers didn't know he could shoot.

"All the hard work, the effort, the blood, sweat, and tears, I couldn't ask for anything more," said Dean Oliver, who was nearing the end of an exceptional four-year career. Iowa earned the Big Ten's automatic NCAA bid and beat Creighton in the first round, 69–56, before losing to Kentucky.

The next season, even with Recker back in the fold and Evans returning, Alford's team didn't have the kind of year many had envisioned. The rest of the squad was loaded with youth and inexperience, and Recker (17.1) and Evans (15.4) were the only ones averaging more than 7 points a game. The Hawks were barely above .500 for the season, finished tied for eighth in the conference and once again were saddled with a Thursday game to begin the postseason tournament. But here is where Recker gave Hawkeye fans some long-lasting memories.

Iowa reeled off victories over Purdue, Wisconsin, and Indiana to reach the title game once more, and it was all because of Recker. In a quarterfinal game against top-seeded Wisconsin, with the score tied at 56–56, Recker swished a fadeaway 15-footer to win the game in the closing seconds. And then in the semifinals, he cut it even closer, releasing his winning 15-foot shot to upset Indiana, 63–61, with only two-tenths of a second showing on the clock.

The fact that he did it against Indiana was doubly sweet for Recker, who said, "I can't describe how good this feels." And Alford was overjoyed, too. "A lot has gone on in his career," said the coach. "This is especially gratifying, knowing what Luke has been through."

Iowa's record of seven consecutive victories in the postseason tournament has not been duplicated and probably won't be for some time. The streak ended there when Ohio State disposed of the Hawks in the championship game. Then they were bounced from the National Invitational Tournament in the first round, losing by 2 points to LSU.

Almost lost in the excitement of Recker's clutch shooting was the work Evans had been doing on the boards, putting some records in the book that also will be hard to match. He had an 18-rebound game against Purdue, tying his mark of the year before, and his 51 rebounds in one tournament, 95 in his two-year career are also records. "Reggie is the best rebounder I've ever coached," says Alford. "He's just a phenomenal athlete. He could go thirty-eight or forty minutes and never get tired. Jeff Horner was a guy who could do that, but very seldom do you find that in a big man."

The end of the line for Recker and Evans ushered in the Jeff Horner-Greg Brunner era. Horner and Brunner were two former Iowa high school stars who became four-year starters. They had known each other since grade school days, when Brunner came from Charles City to attend the basketball camp of Jeff's father,

Mason City High School coach Bob Horner. Their first meeting was not a pleasant one.

"We were in the fifth or sixth grade and both of us were pretty competitive," explained Jeff. "Greg was about the same size as I was back then. We scuffled a bit, and there were some flying elbows and stuff. Later on, we developed a mutual respect for each other. Greg lived only a half hour away from me, and we later played on the same AAU team when we were sophomores in high school."

By that time Horner had already made a verbal commitment to attend Iowa, planning to follow in the path of another of his father's products, Dean Oliver, and he hoped Brunner would join him with the Hawks. "I knew Greg was going to be good, and I remember telling Coach Alford, 'You'd better keep a close eye on him,'" says Jeff.

Both were highly touted all-staters coming out of high school, Horner being honored as Iowa's Mr. Basketball. Brunner had grown into a bruising 6'7", 240-pounder when he and Horner arrived on the Iowa campus in the fall of 2002. They became starters on a young squad that had only one returning regular, guard Chauncey Leslie. The Hawks' 17–14 season ended on a last-second shot by Georgia Tech to beat them in the NIT, 79–78. It started an all-too-familiar pattern.

Their sophomore year was about the same, an overall 16–13 record, and unbelievably, it finished the same way—on another last-second shot, this time by St. Louis, sending Iowa tumbling out of the NIT again, 70–69. Pierce was back in the lineup by then, and with the transfer of Adam Haluska from Iowa State— he had been voted the 2003 freshman of the year in the Big 12—

Alford and the Hawks seemed on the verge of making a major move up in 2005. But that's when Pierce got into trouble again and was kicked off the team. Five losses in six games followed his departure, and although a 21–12 record did get them into the NCAA field, Cincinnati bounced them out in the first round—not by a single point, however. It was 76–64.

While Iowa's football teams were winning and going to January bowl games, basketball enthusiasm was sinking to a new low. Students felt ticket prices were too high, and they found other things to do on game nights. The once-raucous Hawks Nest, a student cheering section, had become conspicuous by its hundreds of empty seats. So that was the picture when Horner and Brunner began their final season.

"The ticket people finally woke up," Horner said. "They lowered the prices so the students felt they could afford to go to more games, and then we started winning. That helped bring more students back and the crowd noise at some of the games was just awesome. They were our sixth man, that's for sure."

Sellout crowds of 15,500 became the norm in early January when the fans discovered what they'd been missing. The Hawks went 17–0 in the home season, the first unbeaten record ever in Carver-Hawkeye Arena, and one of the few in the annals of Iowa basketball. The home finale against Wisconsin, on March 4, was sold out a month in advance.

The season was not without its problems, however. Horner injured a knee in the preconference season and missed four

Doug Thomas (left) and coach Steve Alford hoist the 2006 Big Ten tournament championship trophy. Photo by Harry Baumert, © 2006, The Des Moines Register and Tribune Company. Reprinted with permission.

Fans swing and sway in the Hawks Nest, the Iowa student cheering section.

games. When he returned, he wore a heavy knee brace that curtailed his mobility. Erek Hansen, a 6'11" senior center, was a shot-blocking terror, but he had the disturbing habit of getting into early foul trouble. He was forced to sit out long stretches, letting burly Doug Thomas take over and make some valuable contributions (including a few crowd-pleasing thunder dunks), but Hansen's limited play was impressive enough that he was named the Big Ten's defensive player of the year.

Junior guard Mike Henderson gave the Hawkeyes four native Iowans in the starting lineup for the second year in a row—something that had not happened for three decades. The season appeared to be in danger of capsizing after a humbling 85–55 loss at Michigan State in mid-January, but Iowa rebounded from that by winning four in a row for a 6–2 record in Big Ten games, taking over first place in the conference and holding it for almost five weeks.

When Horner shed his bulky knee brace for a game at Purdue, he caught fire and so did the Hawks. Horner scored a career-high 32 points, hitting 7 of 10 three-pointers to become Iowa's career leader in that category, and the Hawks wiped out a 7-point deficit in the second half to win, 77–68. "I kept telling him to get rid of that brace," quipped Alford.

One of the highlights of the home season was the mid-February rematch with Michigan State, when Horner and Brunner were at their best, each scoring 15 points as the vengeful

Jeff Horner drives in for a layup in a 2006 game. Photo by Harry Baumert, © 2006, The Des Moines Register and Tribune Company. Reprinted with permission.

Hawks once again rallied in the second half to win, 66–54. Horner connected on 3 of 4 three-pointers in one decisive stretch, and he became Iowa's career assist leader in that game. Brunner pulled down 10 rebounds on his way to another career mark. Oldtimers said the crowd noise that night was as loud or louder than they had ever heard for an Iowa home game. "In our first three years, we didn't really have a home-court advantage," said Brunner. "But a lot of credit for our 17–0 home record goes to the fans. That's one thing I'll always remember—the crowd noise on some of those nights."

Iowa finished the regular season with an 11–5 conference record, one game behind champion Ohio State. Brunner led the league in rebounding and became the first Iowa player to make the All-Big Ten first team since Andre Woolridge in 1997. Horner was on the third team, which was probably an oversight, but he left no doubt of his worth in the Big Ten tournament. He played two forty-minute games and totaled 40 points in victories over Minnesota and Michigan State, and then sparked one of Iowa's patented late-game rallies to upset Ohio State for the championship, 67–60. Horner was the obvious choice as the tourney's most outstanding player.

The Hawks appeared ready to make a solid bid in the NCAA tournament, seeded third in their regional—a seeding in postseason play topped only by Iowa's number two seed in 1987. They were paired against thirteenth-seeded Northwestern State of Louisiana in a first-round game at Auburn Hills, Michigan. For almost thirty-two minutes things went the way they were supposed to, but incredibly, in the last 8:29 Iowa blew a 54–37 lead and lost on a last-second three-point shot, 64–63. Shades of the

A "Triple" for the Ages

Jeff Horner left a career record at Iowa after the 2006 season that will be hard to beat. There is no specific record in the Hawkeye book for points-assists-rebounds, but nobody in the past has done what Horner did in four years, and it will probably be a long time before anyone surpasses it.

For years the benchmark has been 1,000 points, 400 assists, and 300 rebounds. The hard part, of course, is to snare a lot of rebounds while also scoring and dishing out assists. Only Dean Oliver, like Horner a product of Mason City High School, managed to top all three of those figures in his four-year career from 1998 to 2001.

Then along came Horner. From his guard position, Jeff pulled down 563 rebounds while scoring 1,502 points and setting a school record with 612 assists. "I know people think a 6'2" point guard shouldn't be getting many rebounds," says Horner, "but I've always had a knack for being around the ball. I think it goes back to playing football and other sports in high school. I always liked to mix it up and go for the ball."

NIT! In three of the four years Horner and Brunner played for Iowa, their seasons finished with 1-point losses in the final second. But that last one really stung.

"That was a terrible way to end a career," said Horner, adding philosophically, "but in thinking about it—and I think about it every five minutes or so—maybe it was fitting. After all the things that had gone wrong for us, you know what they say, whatever can go wrong will go wrong. As impossible as that shot was, maybe it was just meant to be."

Horner and Brunner wound up with almost identical career scoring numbers, Jeff with 1,502 points and Greg 1,516. Each put a school career record in the books—Horner with 612 assists, Brunner with 990 rebounds. Their sterling play won't be soon forgotten.

About the Author

Buck Turnbull is a 1951 graduate of the University of Iowa's School of Journalism. He spent forty-one years as a sportswriter for the *Des Moines Register*, covering many of the games and athletes he writes about in this book. His stories have won numerous awards over the years, and he was twice voted Iowa's sportswriter of the year. He is also the author of *Stadium Stories: Iowa Hawkeyes*, a book on Iowa's NCAA football program.

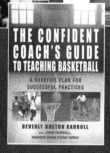